DIVORCE
a challenge to the Church

Text copyright © Bob Mayo 2008
The author asserts the moral right
to be identified as the author of this work

Published by
The Bible Reading Fellowship
15 The Chambers, Vineyard
Abingdon OX14 3FE
United Kingdom
Tel: +44 (0)1865 319700
Email: enquiries@brf.org.uk
Website: www.brf.org.uk

ISBN 978 1 84101 488 3
First published 2008
10 9 8 7 6 5 4 3 2 1 0
All rights reserved

Acknowledgments
Unless otherwise stated, scripture quotations are taken from the Holy Bible, New
International Version, copyright © 1973, 1978, 1984 by International Bible Society, and are
used by permission of Hodder & Stoughton Publishers, a division of Hodder Headline. All
rights reserved. 'NIV' is a registered trademark of International Bible Society. UK trademark
number 1448790.

Scripture quotations taken from The New Revised Standard Version of the Bible, Anglicized
Edition, copyright © 1989, 1995 by the Division of Christian Education of the National
Council of the Churches of Christ in the USA, are used by permission. All rights reserved.

Vows and Partings, Methodist Publishing House, 2001, copyright © TMCP. Used by
permission of the Methodist Publishing House.

A catalogue record for this book is available from the British Library

Printed in Singapore by Craft Print International Ltd

DIVORCE

a challenge to the Church

BOB MAYO

ACKNOWLEDGMENTS

There are a lot of angels busy on my behalf. Thank you to all of you: Edward, David (A-T), Catherine, Courtney, Mummy, Daddy, David (E), Gillian, Louise, Charles and Amanda for unsentimental family pragmatism.

Mummy, Catherine (again), Pip and Femke for arguing me out of myself.

Sarah, happy times none the less; Pamela, dignity; Justin, friendship; Michael, concern; Rick, you were kind; David (C), you minded; Michael and Helen, you empathized; Andy, you talked me through (wit, wisdom and insight!); Simon, you probed; Ed and Modchick, you absorbed; Eve, Addie and Oscar, you accompanied; Jo, you imagined; Ruth, you big-pictured; Sylvie, you know what you mean to me.

CONTENTS

FOREWORD

Marriage has always been important to the Church as a central pillar of Christian living and family life. Many people who believe firmly in the sanctity of marriage today find themselves facing the reality of life as a divorced person. Many also find themselves called, either as pastors or as family and friends, to support and care for people whose marriage has ended.

In this book, Bob Mayo gives us thoughtful and insightful reflections on what it means to be a Christian who upholds the importance of marriage, yet has to face life as a divorced person. His book is no abstract discussion of ideas but a profoundly engaged reflection on the disorientating experience of divorce, seeking strength from struggling with scripture and theology for the journey of life beyond divorce. He gives helpful practical advice to family and friends and to the Church—and a challenge to support people in the transition of divorce.

Bob uses the metaphor of 'exile' to explore how God's presence may be encountered even by those struggling in the wilderness of divorce—and offers hope for new life. In his own words, the author gives us a 'raw, real and authentic' Christianity, which I warmly commend.

+ *Michael Kensington*

INTRODUCTION

The origins of this book lie in the fact that, while coming to terms with my own divorce, I have been met with kindness and confusion in equal measures. People have wanted to help but have been unsure how they might do so. I have written one chapter in direct response to this, entitled 'Dos and Don'ts'. This chapter gives some practical pastoral tips and insights for anyone needing to offer support to someone being divorced. The book provides an extended theological reflection on the reality of divorce and it also makes the case for the church to offer people a specially tailored service that would acknowledge the end of their marriage within a liturgical setting. Other than this, the book furnishes a collective consciousness for people who have been or are being divorced—akin to a 'divorced worldview'.

MY STORY AND I

I have kept a fairly comprehensive journal during my recovery period and I use my personal record of feelings and experiences to guide and sometimes to illustrate the material that follows. This is not always directly acknowledged or apparent but, on occasions, I have found it easiest to make my point by quoting directly from the journal. I made the following entry after a grim New Year's Eve:

My first crisis moment catches me by surprise. It comes unplanned, unexpected and unwelcome. It is New Year's Eve and I am standing on my own, with a pint of beer in my hand, in a city geared for celebration. I had been planning to spend the night with friends. They were planning a dinner party to see in the New Year. It would have been civilized and it would have been fun. However, the hostess rang this morning to say that her husband had been ill during the night and they would need to cancel.

I am determined not to feel sorry for myself so I go for a walk, and so it is that, at 9pm, with the city switching into party gear, I am outside and on my own. The urge to turn and run for home is overwhelming. I can switch on the TV and feel safe. I can watch a film. I can drink; I can smoke; I can do anything except think. I can block out the reality of my situation. I can go to sleep and wake up the next day. There will be no loss of face because no one will ever know that I have been on my own for the evening.

It is then that obstinacy kicks in. I decide to stay where I am. I feel that I have as much right to be outside as any of the happy, smiling couples or the boisterous, extraverted groups of laughing teenagers. I try to convince myself that no one is going to judge me or feel sorry for me because I am standing on my own. They do not know what I am doing and, as far as they are concerned, I might be waiting for someone. I feel lonely, self-conscious and insecure. It is a blisteringly unhappy moment. Strangely, though, I like the fact that, unhappy moment as it is, it is at least *my* unhappy moment. I feel comforted by that thought. In the middle of my feeling grubby, lonely and sad, I feel the glimmerings of a sense of self-respect: I have not scuttled home, turned on the television and tried to block out the reality of what is happening.

It is a dull and unexceptional type of suffering. There is nothing brave about feeling terrified at the prospect of an evening ahead on my own. However, what is significant is that it is the first occasion, since the breakdown of the marriage, when the immediate moment has become more compelling than my endlessly obsessing about all that has happened previously. When the marriage began to unravel, I was completely preoccupied with trying to work out what Sarah wanted and what I should do in response.

As it happens, my nervous sense of social exposure does not last for very long because, after an hour or so, I bump into friends. We spend the rest of the evening together and I return to my house at 1am.

It was not the loudest, wildest, most fun evening of my life, but it was *my* not-so-loud, not-so-fun and not-so-wild evening. I have had the tiniest pinprick of a glimpse of what it means to be able to think for myself—and having done it once, I feel confident that I will be able to do it again.

Using my own story in this way is an important element in making sense of the situation: 'we are our stories'.[1] It lends a sense of context, honesty and authenticity to what would otherwise be a generalized set of conclusions. There is more immediacy to stories that draw from actual events and concrete situations ('What was I doing when…?') rather than hypothetical ones ('What would I do if…?'). In particular, my experience challenges the assumption that divorce, while being a regular occurrence, is still a distant phenomenon, particularly among those in my situation as a church leader.

Stories are the quickest and easiest way of giving you the information you need about everything that happened to me and how I dealt with it all—while leaving you, as the reader, free to form your own conclusions. Stories are tentative and hesitate to draw too bold a set of assertions: they allow you to pre-judge my situation. Pre-judging is different from prejudice. Prejudice is blind and bigoted: it means that someone has decided on an opinion and refuses to budge. Pre-judgment is natural and instinctive: it means that someone has formed an opinion but is happy to see it revised.

'How can I give an opinion when I do not have all the facts?' my father would ask of me, with the forensic precision typical of a lawyer of his calibre. I would reply that even if he had all the facts I would still need his opinion because I would want to know how to connect all the facts together. My stories give you the gaps between the different facts and help you to imagine yourself into my situation.

'Judge a person by his shoes,' my grandmother always told me. It is the glimpse of other people's lives that helps us to shape the instinctive pre-judgment we make of any situation. You as the reader need my stories not so that you can sit in judgment on Sarah and me but so that you can shape your pre-judgments, which will in turn shape the ultimate conclusions you draw from the book.

A SURVIVOR

The etymology of the word 'survivor' is to 'live above'. This offers a more dynamic sense to the word than the dull idea of survival as nothing more than continuing to exist and clinging on. Divorce, remarriage and children born out of wedlock have become so well established in British life that special greeting cards are designed to celebrate the complex relationships that typify 21st-century families: 'To Mummy and Daddy on your wedding day'; 'Happy Christmas to Mum and boyfriend'. As well as 'egreetings', there are 'dgreetings' that one partner in a divorce can send to the other: 'My heart mourns at the fact that the spark of love that ignited passion in our soul can't be rekindled again' (www.dgreetings.com). In addition, the Yorkshire Building Society offers a 'Fresh Start' mortgage tailored to people coming out of a messy break-up or divorce. All these are expressions of the ability of human beings to 'live above' their situation and move forward in it.

My experiences are unique and specific to me; at the same time, they are illustrative of the experience of the divorced ten per cent of the UK population. Every experience of the end of a relationship is distinctive, different and 'other'; however, a broken heart is a broken heart whatever the circumstances behind it. I hope, therefore, that this book will be relevant to anyone going through the experience and in whatever way—whether as the one leaving or the one left. The person who ends the relationship may feel an immediate relief but a subsequent guilt. By contrast, the person who is left may feel immediate grief but then less guilt. There are themes that are common to all—vulnerability, social isolation and the consequent spiritual and emotional exposure, which put people in need of protection and direction from the church. An extract from my journal illustrates these themes:

I am living on the edge of other people's rituals—children's christenings, weddings, birthdays, even funerals. I stand and I watch, I listen and I talk. I ask questions and I make comments. I am serious, solemn or jocular according to what the other person is saying. Listening is all I can do because, at the moment, I have got nothing to say. People talk to me because they can see that I want to listen.

I ask couples about where they first met. It is a good question for me to ask because they will take a while to reply. The longer they talk, the less I need to talk, and at the moment that suits me fine. Couples with tired marriages, who have been together for ten and twenty years, tell me with a twinkle in their eyes about how they first met. Older people introduce me to their younger, cheeky selves; younger people give me a glimpse of the sombre, solemn, hopeful person lying within.

I talk about them because I am happy not to talk about myself. I am able to see and understand more about people's lives precisely because I am lying outside their regular, structured narrative of events. I am 'poor in spirit' (Matthew 5:3) because I have nothing that I want to add to the conversation. The less that I bring of myself, the more I seem to appreciate what others tell of themselves. I am the man with no name, the man without a story because, as my hopes for the future are disintegrating, my understanding of the past evaporates.

Despite these common emotions, I am not suggesting that my experiences should provide a standard template for how to deal with divorce. The other side of the coin, as I have mentioned, is the unique and distinctive nature of each person's situation. This needs careful handling on my part and discerning reading on yours. I am in a good position to write this book because I have my own set of experiences to draw from, but I do not want to use the fact that I have been divorced as an emotional trump card to claim legitimacy for what I have to say; the ending of a marriage is not a triumphant story. My stories provide authenticity rather than authority to my treatment of the subject—a way of considering the wider context of the debate.

I feel a fierce loyalty to those people described elsewhere in the book as the 'society of the dispossessed'. They have had their marriage snatched away and should not now have their individual story removed by the colonizing words of someone such as myself who has chosen to go to print. There is a blurred line between the author's 'could be' and the reader's interpretation as 'should be'. My way of coping with divorce may not be theirs. This book is not a recovery manual but one person's fumbling attempts to draw away from the collapse of their marriage.

We all have our own way of dealing with things, and the subconscious does its own work, as the following extract from my journal demonstrates:

I had a dream about Sarah. She had died and I was griefstruck—there were things that had not been said and I felt that I needed to be there with her family. Concerned Christians who thought that I should not go were smothering me. They took me on a bus but it was going in the wrong direction. I ran to get on a bus that was travelling back in the direction I had just come from. Once on the bus, I recognized Sarah's brother Peter. Sitting crosslegged on the dashboard was Sarah's mother, going through all the arrangements that needed to be done. They were pleased to see me because Sarah had left in her will that I should be included in the service and they did not know how they were going to manage that.

My way of coping is to write, read, run or watch films. I always run an identical route at a set and regular pace, with the very same music playing each time, and there is a point in the route where the rhythm of the music, my steps as I run and the beat of my heart are perfectly synchronized. These are welcome points of momentary anaesthesia, which help to start the process of building blocks of new experience as a counterweight to my divorce. I watch bland 'chewing-gum' television programmes with whipped-up plots and improbable characters. I read trashy, repetitive books (thrillers with clumsy storylines and predictable outcomes)—anything not to have to think. In the first instance, I want to shut my mind to the full reality of the situation.

Inevitably, this emotional prevarication is more about postponement than about moving on with a finishing process. Looking at what has happened through filtered lenses is an early stage in the grieving process. In time I will work through the Kübler-Ross five stages of grief. 'Denial' will eventually lead into 'anger', 'bargaining', 'depression' and finally 'acceptance'.[2] People can help me but no one can hurry the process. The grieving process is akin to Godard's celebrated dictum about a film—that it must have a beginning, a middle and an end, but not necessarily in that order.[3]

I find that I am for ever stumbling over people's assumption that I should be talking about my feelings as a way of coming to terms with the situation. However, talking simply makes me feel that I am reliving everything that has happened, and I end up feeling doubly traumatized by it all. I am not trying to draw all-purpose principles from this tight, 'male' coping strategy, but it suits me in the early stages of my recovery process.

The Bible has a tradition of giving honour and respect to outsiders, people who don't fit. The Psalms talk of God's special care for widows, aliens (strangers) and orphans (see 68:5; 146:9), and a modern version of this list might include divorced people. This scriptural respect is not a consolation prize for those of us who seem to have missed out on everything else. It is a description of how things actually are: I am blessed through what has happened because, although misery is a hard taskmaster, it offers clarity and insight and understanding. Now that I feel truly unhappy, I have no space to defend. Divorce has given me a set of insights and learning about life that I would never otherwise have had. I can already see glimpses of things that I might have to offer other people as a result.

The fact that I am suffering means that I am able to offer reassurance to others; it is the oppressed who make the first move, the afflicted person who offers comfort and sustenance. These are hard-won insights.

A SENSE OF IMMEDIACY

Although the events I refer to in this book are now some years past, the sense of immediacy that I want to convey is emphasized by my use of the historic present and the first person 'I' rather than the third person 'he' throughout. My ex-wife, as you will have noticed, is referred to throughout as Sarah (which is a pseudonym). Divorce is a jarring, disabling experience, and I want to reflect some of this jitteriness back to you by presenting events as if they were happening now.

I have talked with a number of people about their particular experiences of divorce. Their comments are included in the book, along with my own experiences, as illustrative material. There is a part-anonymity offered to these people: their comments are not always individually identified and are sometimes included as part of a composite picture.

Drawing from other people's stories as well as my own allows a voice to the diversity and the fragmented nature of divorce. The fact that my story is different from another person's can be a strength rather than a weakness. Storytelling is more collage than photograph: it avoids a single generalized framework of interpretation and allows expression to the voices of different people. As Leo Tolstoy wrote in *Anna Karenina*, 'Happy families are all alike; every unhappy family is unhappy in its own way.'[4] For example, Sarah and I never had children. Part of my recovery has come because I have been able to cut contact with her, and I would not have had this choice if we had had children together. This means that I can give limited attention to the effect that divorce might have on children. Annie, who contributed to the 'Dos and Don'ts' chapter, writes as a mother with children, while the chapter on 'The family' draws on material looking at the effect divorce can have on children.

The following are examples of things that people have told me about their experience of divorce.

- Each day was a hard fight against sliding downhill into self-pity and depression.
- Some people just become drained of life: I also just couldn't go out because I didn't have the energy. I could just about go to work, but that was it. It was so surprising, because I was still quite young—I was only 35 and I'd had tons of energy before.
- Once the initial intensity of grief has subsided and the reality of the situation has sunk in, then divorce is about coping from day to day, week to week, year to year. That coping may take various forms. Very often it means immersing oneself in work or family.
- To begin with, in England, I just worked. I was working seven-day weeks—80 hours a week. I just worked—that's what I did.
- How I describe it is, it's like, every morning you get up, you put the 60lb pack on, you climb up the mountain, you climb back down again, and then the next day you've gotta do it again… and again… and again. And all that you're conscious of is that you've got to keep doing it, and it's hard graft.

There is a hard emotional slog needed to get through the experience of divorce. Other comments made to me are about how children provide a focus of attention. Concentrating on their immediate needs is a way of negotiating the transitions needing to be faced.

- Nevertheless, children provide a spur and an incentive to carry on when there is little other inducement. When there are children to be fed and watered, the show must go on.
- With children, you've got to go on. They don't give you any option. You plough on.

- But however much I didn't feel like going on, I knew I had to go on because these three guys [the children] were depending on me.

The strongest picture, however, is simply of people who were unhappy.

- I moved through a number of phases—at first, griefstricken, initially for the loss of the girl I loved as much for the loss of the marriage. I remember talking to my sister on the phone, and saying, 'Why? Why? Why?'
- The pavements between here and the Co-op are marked with my unhappiness and anger and bitterness and upset.

When there are children in the marriage, this adds another layer of distress and tragedy. Those who are parents typically describe the breaking up of the family as the most painful part.

- Wherever I went, the world seemed to be full of families, out together, just being together, bickering, teasing, joking, dads taking their weekend turn with the pushchair, doing everyday stuff. It drove a dagger into my heart. We would never, never be a family like that again. What have I done to my child, that she would never know this everyday security? What careless choices of mine have denied her this?
- I grieved for the loss of my family. I had my family, my wife and my children... and that was shattered. I was very fortunate in that I was kept so busy. I felt suicidal—but didn't get close to actually planning it.

THE CASE FOR A LITURGY OF TRANSITION

There are a lot of divorced people sitting in church pews and, in cases like mine, even preaching from behind church lecterns. The question I am asking is how the church might best be able to provide a consistent, well-informed and pastorally sensitive response to those of us who have been divorced. There are two central thoughts in this book. The first is that the idea of being in exile can be used as a metaphor for divorce; the second is that the church should be offering to people who have been divorced some structured opportunity for regret, remorse and repentance for the past, along with forgiveness, hope and promise for the future. This could be done either through specially tailored prayers or through a liturgical service of healing for those whose marriage is ending or has ended.

My argument is that a service of closure would not legitimate divorce. It is possible for the church to be accepting of those who are dealing with the consequences while still being clear about the inherent wrongness of divorce. My suggestion is that a liturgy of transition could become one among a range of options offered by the church. The prayers at the end of this book are an example of something of this type. The prayers, written through the Methodist Church, are appropriate either to a divorce or to the ending of a love affair.

The Anglican Churches in Canada and Australia have produced a liturgical service to mark the end of a marriage, but an attempt to do something similar by the United Reformed Church (URC) in England in 1993 was met with a degree of hostility and criticism. Among the wider church leadership, this opposition may have stemmed from unwillingness to be publicly associated with an issue that would offend religious sensibilities. Among divorced lay people, it may have been linked with a lack of ownership of the issue, due to feelings of shame[5] and a desire to distance themselves from the experience. (I look in detail elsewhere in the book at the idea of shame and divorce: shamed people are less likely to want to bring attention on themselves.)

Other reasons for this hostility towards the idea of a liturgy of transition may have emerged from a misconception of the role of

Christian theology in public life. Public theology is not simply a set of propositions saying that something is either right or wrong; it is a way of interpreting the world in the light of a belief in God. A liturgy of transition neither exonerates nor condemns what has happened; it offers me a way of making sense of and coming to terms with what is happening. I can't undivorce myself, so what I need from theology is not simply an application of biblical truths to my life but an integration between my Christian faith and the reality of my situation. It is not inconsistent for the church to recognize both that divorce is wrong and that dealing with divorce is un-avoidable.

Nevertheless, there has been a significant shift in the way the church relates to people who have been divorced. The Church of England General Synod recognized that while '"marriage should always be undertaken as a solemn, public and life-long covenant between a man and a woman"; there are circumstances in which a divorced person may be married in church during the lifetime of a former spouse'.[6]

The logic that allows a second wedding service for some people who have been divorced should also allow a liturgy of transition for those either unwilling or unable to remarry. At the moment, ritual acknowledgment of the end of a marriage comes only with the arrangements for a second marriage. There is no liturgical service offering any form of closure to the divorced person who is either unable or not intending to marry again and instead wants to live a celibate, single life after the ending of their marriage.

Some people are not given the gift of marriage: they live challenging, sometimes difficult and often fulfilled lives as single people. Some people are given the gift of marriage and they cultivate it and watch it grow. Others, such as myself, are given the gift of marriage and squander it. The question in this book is how the church can reflect God's compassion and forgiveness, yet stand firm on the sanctity of marriage and the vows of lifelong commitment. What is the best way for the church to acknowledge my situation as a divorced person without appearing to condone the end of my marriage? Beck-Gernsheim says that the normalization of fragility is what lies ahead for the family; she describes it as a tacit normalization of divorce.[7] How can the church acknowledge the pastoral needs of those within this situation while also interpreting and challenging the social trends that created those needs?

A part of the answer to this question will come through un-blocking people's nervousness when asked to care pastorally for someone going through a divorce. It is a big jump to go from knowing someone as part of a married couple to relating to them as a divorced, single person. I am looking to the church for comfort and support but often find myself frozen solid in a pastoral no-man's land. People who have been friends to Sarah and me as a couple are struggling to learn how to relate to us as individuals. They have had to reposition themselves in our lives just as we have had to in each other's life. Some people don't know whether to support us or challenge us. Some, who want to remain friends to both of us, get drawn in and suffer as collateral damage. Divorce not only breaks the bedrock teaching of the church about the family, but it also undercuts the organization of churches around the ideal of a happy and united family.

I hope that my use of exile as a metaphor for divorce will prevent you, the reader, from simply feeling sorry for me as someone who has been divorced. I have no desire for divorced people to be treated as a new oppressed minority within the church, added to the list of people feeling marginalized or hard done by. I do not want to 'champion the cause' of the divorced. In almost any subset within the church—singles, teens, older people, homosexuals, childless couples or clergy—there will be some who feel that the church is not geared to them and their particular needs. This book is not trying to make any kind of rallying call on behalf of any one of these groups. Happily married couples with children can just as easily feel taken for granted as single people in a church programme where too many of the jobs are done by too few of the people. The reality of church life is that the consumers outnumber the producers.

I do not intend this book to be seen as undercutting the centrality of marriage within the Christian tradition. The damaging effects of divorce and the value of a stable marriage are self-evident. At the same time, I do not want the church to make a scapegoat of divorced people to reinforce the importance of marriage. Thatcher warns against a teaching on marriage (and families) that derives entirely from a prior concern to defend nuclear families.[8] All societies tend to exclude various groups of people, making them victims, so that those who are on the 'inside' have something by which to measure their own sense of success and self-worth.

A liturgy of transition would sit in an institutional blind spot for the church: an organization that gears its strategy towards avoiding divorce does not easily form a response should that situation arise. As I have already stated, however, doctrinal correctness over the centrality of marriage need not be compromised by a finely tuned pastoral response to those whose marriage has ended. Christians are called to be people of grace *and* truth. If I am offered too much grace and acceptance, then forgiveness becomes condoning, emotion becomes sentimentality and my divorce is seen as being unfortunate rather than wrong. If I am offered too much truth, judgment becomes condemnation and the possibility of redemption is squeezed out of the whole process. I don't want other people to pretend that everything is all right; equally, I don't want to be made to feel worse than I already do.

The law has ended my marriage but now I need the church to help me to finish it. The distinction between 'ending' and 'finishing' can be illustrated by reference to a dinner party. People might arrive for the meal at 8pm and leave at 10.30. The dinner ends when the last guest leaves, but it will not have properly finished until I have cleared the table and washed up. Practical, pragmatic law courts are the only social narrative of explanation for the end of a marriage; but it was in church that my marriage began and it is through the church that any finishing must come. Divorce is distinctive because once it has happened it can't be undone simply through regret and repentance. Finishing will come when I have been able to work through all the implications and fallout from my divorce.

Jesus' teaching about the danger of leaving a house empty (Luke 11:24–26) can refer to the danger of leaving a difficult situation in limbo. A vacuum never remains as such but will be filled with competing forces so that the person ends up worse off than they were before. A liturgy of transition will not plug the emotional gaps, nor will it mend the sacramental shredding wrought by divorce. What it will do is to offer a holding station where divorced people can seek the protective and healing cover of the church. It is more akin to a Noah's ark (in other words, a transitional place) than to a temple (that is, a permanent home). When Joshua crossed the River Jordan into the promised land, he set down twelve stones to mark the transition from the old to the new (Joshua 4:19–24), and this signified both a completion and a new beginning. I would like a similar transition marker for my own life.

A liturgy of transition per se could be just as pertinent to any change in a situation that defines a person's own sense of identity. Negative experiences such as divorce, unemployment or a miscarriage—as well as positive experiences such as the birth of a child or moving house—can all have the same effect of dislocation and loss of identity. In the UK, theology does not yet see itself on the same shelf as the self-help books written to offer top tips on life-changing situations, but there is no reason why the church, as a body of believers, should not draw on the treasury of its accumulated wisdom and offer insights to those people who might be glad for a sense of direction and don't want to wait until Sunday to receive it. A liturgy of transition would also offer an opportunity for the church, as an institution, to reconnect with citizens in their day-to-day living and re-establish trust among people who would otherwise be feeling disenfranchised.

EXILE

This book constructs a theological framework round the destruction of Jerusalem in 587BC and the Israelites' subsequent exile in Babylon. Divorce and exile are mapped on to each other in three different ways. The fall of Jerusalem is used as a parallel to the collapse of my marriage, the period in exile is used as a parallel to the period of readjustment after my divorce, and the eventual return to Jerusalem is used to parallel a final process of recovery. The question of how to sing in a strange and difficult land (Psalm 137:4) is adopted as a guiding question to the process of seeking healing and recovery.

The idea of exile can be used as a metaphor not only for divorce but also for Christian living more generally, and can be understood positively as well as negatively. Exile is a hopeful image of growth and potential as well as a negative image involving ideas of distance, alienation and separation, being away from home, excluded and unable to return. When the Israelites were exiled from Jerusalem, they were in both a religious and a geographical wilderness, and they found that this wilderness was not simply a transitory state that finished once they returned home. After they returned to Jerusalem, it was the wilderness and the lessons they learnt while in exile, rather than the temple and their previous religious practice, that shaped how they understood God.

I draw from the work of Walter Brueggeman and track the same questions asked of the exiled Israelites by the psalmist. What is the significance of their previous life in Jerusalem? How do their memories of Jerusalem shape the understanding they have of themselves and what role do these memories play in their new life in Babylon? The answer is that their Jerusalem memories remind the Israelites that although they have become a part of Babylonian culture, they do not belong there because they have a distinctive identity as the people of God. They are not simply a vanquished and scattered diaspora, and this means that remembering their past is key to retaining their identity as the people of God. If they forget

Jerusalem, then they will become absorbed into the Babylonian culture. If they cling to memories of Jerusalem, however, then they will be unable to engage with the Babylonian culture and get on with their lives. They will be unable to do what the prophet Jeremiah asks of them, which is to live out the reality of their new situation and seek the peace and prosperity of the city to which God has taken them into exile (Jeremiah 29:7).

Using my own experience of divorce, I cast myself as the person in exile. I ask the same question of my situation that the Israelites asked of theirs. What is the significance of my past life as a married man? How do my memories of marriage and divorce shape the understanding I have of myself, and what role do these memories play in my new life? The answer is that allowing myself to live with both the grief that is now, and the happiness that was in my now-ended marriage, offers me my only opportunity for integrity and wholeness. If I try to deny what my marriage meant to me, I become a half-person, shutting my mind to what has happened in the past. I end up either apathetic or hedonistic, because all I have to live in is the immediate and present moment. If I try to hide myself in nostalgia for the past, however, again I shrivel, shutting my mind both to what is happening now and to what might happen in the future. I become either bitter (if I blame my ex-wife) or melancholic (if I blame myself).

My dilemma is similar to the one faced by the Israelites. This book adopts the idea of the Israelites learning to sing the Lord's song in a strange land as a paradigm both for the Christian's involvement in contemporary society and for the divorced person's recovery from the breakdown of their marriage. The writer of Psalm 137 asks how this can be done, as both a therapeutic and a theological question. First, it is therapeutic because the psalmist is distraught. There is a brutal passage within the psalm, singing to God for deliverance but also longing for the violent deaths of his enemies' children (v. 9). Verses of expectation, longing and love hold within them the apparently opposite sentiments of hate, revenge and bloody-mindedness. The two emotions are not mutually exclusive. Second, the question is theological because the Israelites no longer have access to the temple in Jerusalem and have to learn new ways of worshipping Yahweh. In the same way, in my situation I need both therapy and theology. I have to deal with my anger as well as reshape my understanding of what faith in God will mean to me now that I am divorced and in exile.

The power of the image of the Israelites sitting by the rivers in Babylon is in the strange, eerie sadness, where melancholic feelings of loss and longing run in parallel with violent and angry reactions towards those who are causing the pain. This melancholy allied to the untrammelled violence in the language provides a perfect reflection of myself. At the same time, it cradles my imagination and demands an alternative world of hope and possibility because, in his grief, the psalmist recognizes that, just as things have changed once, they will need to change again. Christianity is not about forgetting but about remembering well. Forgiveness does not mean pretending that nothing bad has happened. It means acknowledging, understanding and then forgiving. This is a work of grace that keeps me from being trapped by what has happened. Part of the curious nature of redemption is that it is when people are at their lowest ebb that they receive promises, energy and empowerment from God.

The point of remembering well is not to convince myself that the world is a safe place and I have nothing to fear but to prepare myself to live again in a frightening world that has hurt me badly. Remembering well makes me realize that, since things have collapsed once, they could all too easily collapse again. If my life can be changed as completely as it has over the last few years, what is to say that it might not happen again? It is this realization that teaches me to care passionately and fight tenaciously for my future; grief expresses itself through hope.

TO CONCLUDE

Divorce has taken my spiritual and emotional virginity. Before the fall broke the covenant between God and humankind, 'what is' and 'what ought to be' were the same thing, but now, after the fall, they are separate. Before my divorce I was 'naked but not ashamed' (Genesis 2:25): 'naked' not in the sense that I was perfect but that I had nothing to be ashamed of. I was imperfect but free from fear of disapproval. Now that my divorce has broken my marriage covenant, I am still 'naked' but now I want to hide. I ruminate on all sorts of lurid narratives to try to put what has happened into context. I feel like the elder brother in the story of the good Samaritan (Luke 15:25–28), who stands to one side while his younger brother is welcomed home. I imagine the story of someone who has been a drug dealer, shot someone, then been converted and become a Christian. He could be speaking at a Christian conference within six months, telling people the story of how Christ saved him. My situation is that I had been going to church for ten years and then got divorced—I simply end up feeling ashamed.

There is a thin dividing line between too much and too little information about myself: stories of how much I am struggling to get my life back on track might be interesting but not always informative. If the focus of this book falls more on me and my feelings than on divorce and its social implications, then the book will end up as a deliberate, self-conscious pathology, an extended example of 'woundology', described by Myss as the sharing of wounds, the new language of intimacy, a short cut to developing trust and understanding.[9] There are two traps in 'woundology', both of which I want to avoid. The first trap is to substitute feeling for understanding. This book has been written to give you a vicarious insight into the experience of being divorced, and this is a task of the mind as well as the heart. The second trap is definition by default. 'Woundology' would mean defining myself by what has gone wrong, and all you would be given is the chance to learn what a terrible time I have been having. My challenge is to allow myself to be defined by Christ's redemption rather than by the misery of all that has happened.

Everyone likes a happy story. There is a standard 'rom-com' film narrative about what happens when relationships break up: things are difficult for a period but come right in the end when the hero(ine) falls in love again and lives happily ever after. If I tell my story with a simple, two-dimensional 'Then I was sad but now I am happy' twist, then I can leave you, as the reader, feeling excluded in one of two ways. If you are struggling in your own life, you might feel alienated by a book with too strong a 'happy ever after' storyline. If you are happy, and interested only to find out more about divorce, you might feel excluded from a storyline that speaks too strongly of difficult situations producing illuminating insights. I have read some books that have left me feeling disempowered because of the implicit suggestion that the worse the experience, the more we learn about how to appreciate life—as if we need to have experienced Sarajevo in the middle of the civil war in order to have a rounded view of life.

The idea that divorce is my crucifixion and a future happiness will be my resurrection is theologically glib because it sees crucifixion and resurrection as being entirely sequential (one coming after the other) rather than simultaneous (one blending into the other). Before his crucifixion, Jesus made explicit references to the kingdom of God as having already arrived (Mark 1:15) and yet being still on its way (9:1). The kingdom of God is not a process that waits until Jesus has been crucified before it kicks in. After Jesus' resurrection, Paul and the apostles saw the crucifixion as the core part of the message they had to offer (1 Corinthians 1:23). For the apostles, crucifixion was not something that they left behind as they moved on. It became an integral part of who they were together.

A book that conformed too closely to this stylized 'happy ever after' social narrative would be read as a morality tale describing how things should have been as much as how things actually were.

Trying to parcel divorce entirely within such standardized categories of interpretation is reminiscent of Canute trying to hold back the waves with his hands. It ignores the jerky, disjointed and destructive nature of the experience. It is reversion therapy—a 'back to the basics' family message. It also ignores the fact that the prevalence of divorce is reshaping our understanding of family life. I look elsewhere at how the shape of a family can no longer be taken for granted, and cannot even necessarily be measured against the benchmark of a two-parent nuclear family. Some aspects of divorce are not simply evidence of the breakdown of society but can also be seen as part of a process of society renewing and transforming itself.

LIVING IN EXILE

THE INSTINCT TO MAKE SENSE OF THINGS

I am leading a class for Reception and Year 1 in the local primary school. We are in church, doing a picture treasure hunt in which the children are given photographs of different objects in the church and have to try to find them. When they leave, one child says to me, 'I am so… proud'; a second one looks at me and says, 'I love you'; a third child goes through and says, 'Goodbye, Potato Head.' They are children, aged only five and six, and each of them is putting their experience into a set of words that makes sense to them. At primary school age, children tend to think in concrete rather than abstract conceptual terms, so they test out ideas to see how well or otherwise they match with an experience.

This is not dissimilar to the way we live our lives as adults. How people make sense of being divorced is shown in the way that they describe it. Some people talk of being divorced as a condition: 'I have been divorced for *[x]* years.' Others talk of being divorced as a moment in time: 'I was divorced on *[a particular date]*.' Each sentence gives a significant and different interpretation of the experience.

Feeling the need to make some sort of sense of our lives is a human characteristic. We are continually taking stock, reappraising and reassessing in order to make stories of our lives that have meaning. We all have our own ways of making sense of things—our version of the children saying, 'I am so… proud', 'I love you' or 'Goodbye, Potato Head'. When something difficult, painful or unexpected happens, we hold on to what we know and wrestle with what we do not understand. We are reassured by boundaries and definitions and so we instinctively try to put events into a familiar framework so that we can understand them. Divorce stripped away my marriage, which was one seemingly categorical framework, and left me struggling to find a new framework that will fit better with my situation. This is illustrated by the panic I feel when I am confronted at a party by different versions of the same scenario.

'Are you married?' someone asks me. 'No, I am divorced,' I reply, and then I begin to worry. I have not answered the question I was asked. He simply wanted to know whether I was married or not and I have answered by telling him I am divorced. Have I given him too much information? Will he mind? Does it matter? Am I using these types of conversations to help me understand and get used to my new reality? If this is the case, then I am demanding a lot from people. There is no reason why they should even begin to be able to guess at what I am feeling.

Divorce feels like a brand on my forehead. It has catapulted me into situations where I have to learn whole new ways of being in the world and engaging with people. Old certainties have gone and simple social encounters can leave me panic-stricken. Am I now stuck with this situation? Is it best to volunteer the information about my divorce straight away—as a kind of pre-emptive strike—rather than letting people find out at a later date and perhaps judge me more harshly as a result?

I made the following recording in my journal:

I am the dreamer who has tripped clumsily over his own two feet: the emotional vagabond, frightened at long evenings and Sunday afternoons on my own, scared at the thought of parties and gatherings where well-intentioned people would ask me if I am married. Maybe I am now only ever going to feel comfortable with those who themselves have been through a divorce? I call us the 'society of the dispossessed': people with a shared set of experiences that do not need any explanation.

I have been the outsider all year, since I learnt the situation between us. I am living in one town and working in another. I get out of bed in London while it is still dark. I travel to Cambridge, where I am now working, and I arrive before people have even started their lecture programme for the day. On one occasion I travelled for two hours for a meeting that was due to start at 9am. It was cancelled because some student on campus had agreed at short notice to take his children to school. I am there but I am not there. I do not go to the staff meetings. I rarely go to the chapel and if I eat in College it is only because I am going in with someone from outside.

I go for runs across the meadow in the late afternoon before I catch a train back to London. As I run, I play loud, banging club music, grating in my ears. The beat of club music is always consciously set faster than the beat of a heart, so it jars the rhythmic quality of a steady breathing synchronized with my running movement. The run becomes a race, with me wanting only to cover the ground quicker than I might have done before.

Each week has been a waiting for the weekend, and each weekend is a similar lethargic marking of time until the beginning of the next week. A film or the omnibus edition of a soap opera is fine, but it finishes at 6.30, so what happens then? At the weekends I try to convince myself that longer in bed means more rest. Why not lie in bed and listen to *The Archers* on Sunday morning? *Desert Island Discs* is the next programme on the radio, and that is nice to listen to as well. Artificial, unexciting, self-created pegs mark the progress of the weekend. It is limbo land and I wait week after week for something to happen. I measure out the minutes of the day with nervous introspection. A tense and pallid smile is there to hide my lack of hope. I am de-manned. I want my life back—tiny, drab and uninviting it may be, but at least it is mine.

People ask me how I am.

So again I run. This time it is along the banks of the river Thames. Across Tower Bridge, past the Tower of London, St Paul's Cathedral, Big Ben and the Houses of Parliament along the north side of the river; then back along the south side—Shakespeare's Globe and Southwark Cathedral—beautiful, pale early evening sky, the river trigger-sensitive to the changing weather, the hordes of city people fading with the light. To end my year, all I want to do is to run. To run a full marathon in a strange city would be perfect. I don't want to run timid five-mile canters. I want to run myself into and beyond exhaustion—and so I do.

I run through the first springy steps of freshness. I run through the careful steeling of the body's momentum. I run into and beyond feeling tired and I run into and beyond aching, cramped limbs. I run on and beyond what my body is capable of doing. Gradually my every bone starts screaming out with agony; my head is giddy and sick with the effort of keeping going; my stomach is parched and shrivelled, burning off any fluid that I have drunk. A mile later, at the last watering station of the marathon, I vomit up what little water and solids I have left inside. It has been my one true act of communion this year.

THEOLOGY: A DIALOGUE BETWEEN SCRIPTURE AND DIVORCE

I need my Christian faith more than I have ever done before, to help me steer a way through this twilight period. The idea that I am in exile, both as a Christian and as someone who is recently divorced, resonates with my situation. The idea of exile offers a dialogical rather than a propositional idea of truth that comes out of the interplay between Christian theology and a particular set of experiences; theology is able to dialogue with and not simply dictate to my situation.

Thinking solely in terms of theological 'right and wrong' creates a need for repentance and change. Yet I can repent all I want, but I will still be divorced. I can't undo what has happened. It is not just a question of my feeling but of actually being divorced. If my theology is simply going to judge me for what I have done wrong, it will not help me, because I am not in a position to undo what has happened.

Theological dialogue, by contrast, is loving, humble, hopeful, trusting and critical.[1] Dialogue means understanding: memories are neither denied nor allowed to dominate. Moreover, transformation will come out of two separate dialogues happening simultaneously.

One dialogue is internal: it is myself understanding, accepting and adjusting to what has happened. The other is external, connecting the disparate set of events that make up my situation with insights and truths from scripture.

Dialogue with myself

The transfiguration (Luke 9:28–36) is the pivotal point of Jesus' ministry. Peter has confessed that Jesus is the Christ (9:20) and now Jesus turns towards Jerusalem. Moses and Elijah appear alongside Jesus, giving him a glimpse of the heavenly glory that lies ahead. The disciples are sleepy and almost miss what is happening: their impressions of the transfiguration are blurred. For Jesus, both the future and the past come into play here. The transfiguration is the point at which he gets a glimpse of what lies ahead, while at the same time being reminded of his past in the shape of Moses and Elijah. Like the transfiguration, divorce is a hinge moment in which the immediate here-and-now is disjointed and both the past and the future come into play. Even when Peter wakes up and sees Moses, Elijah and Jesus together, he does not grasp what is happening. Similarly, I am too busy coping with events to wonder at their significance. Peter wants to build three tents to capture the moment. My three tabernacles are not to prolong the moment but to try to protect myself from it. I am not building—I am hiding.

I have three separate and overlapping identities: there is myself as I was, during and before my marriage; there is myself as I am, shattered by all that has happened; and there is myself as I will be, at the moment glimpsed and only ever imagined. Ideally, memories of my past would blend with an experience of the present and shape my hopes for the future. In reality, the painful nature of what has happened in the past colonizes a pale and insipid immediacy and leaves me feeling glum and feeling pretty hopeless about the future. The easiest thing to do seems to be to try to keep these identities completely separate—but this leads me to one of two extremes. I either shut the door and remain miserable on my own, hiding with my tormenting thoughts of the past, or else I come out and play, defiantly and bravely 'fine' in the company of others. In the former instance, I am allowing the collapse of my marriage to dominate my thoughts; in the latter, I am trying to deny it, shut it out and live my present reality for all it is worth (not that this is always so grim— I can surprise myself by laughing!).

The path that I need to take lies between these two extremes of denial and domination: my past and my present must talk with each other in reasoned tones. The danger of denial is to try to move on too quickly from what has happened; the danger of domination is to make too little attempt to move on. The former leads to apathy and the latter to cynicism.

Apathy comes when I give up trying to come to terms with what has happened and consequently take too little responsibility for my divorce. It is a form of self-denial, a refusal to engage with the reality of the past. When I try to brushstroke out what has happened, I end up with a lack of perspective. My behaviour lurches between apathy ('So what?') and self-indulgence ('Who cares?'). If I have no loyalty to the past, I will have limited energy for the present and I am left feeling unwilling to forgive ('Why do I need to?'). Trivializing the past leaves me feeling dull and hopeless. I have to convince myself that I am over 'it' and that I have put 'it' behind me—'Move on and forget what has happened'— but in reality there is scant consolation in such bullish sentiments.

I spent an evening with one person who was in this position, clearly accepting too little responsibility for his divorce. He was blaming his wife for what she did to him and seeing the breakdown in his marriage as entirely her fault. It was a curious type of self-indulgence to think in the way he did. The emotional logic was that if he had no responsibility in one situation, then why should he have responsibility in another? It meant that he felt he could say or do things without thinking through the consequences. If someone invited him to a party, he might turn up late or not at all. Why not? It made him both attractive and infuriating. He blamed others for what had happened and so saw no reason why he should not now enjoy himself. He was behaving recklessly, with a self-indulgence tinged by apathy. 'So what, what the heck, who cares?'

The second danger, the danger of domination, is the temptation to dwell too deeply on all that has happened. If I do this, I end up cynical and jaundiced. I cling to the memories of the past and convince myself that nothing will ever get any better. I become tied into a cycle of limited expectations, which drains hope and energy from everything else. It feels as if I am locked into a chain of events that will inexorably take their course. I continually go over what happened and think how I might have done things differently. I find it hard to move on and put the past behind me. It is a nagging, crabby, blaming state of mind—a loss of confidence. I lose my nerve and feel low, depressed and lethargic. Being a prisoner to the past makes the present seem empty and meaningless; I am immersed in self-pity, feeling hard done by and, again, unable to forgive ('Why should I?'). I may wear the social mask of someone who is coping but, in reality, I cannot see the situation getting any better.

So, with both of these two extremes, I am caught between 'the devil and the deep blue sea'. I don't want to move on from my marriage, yet at the same time I have no choice but to do so. The temptation is to live entirely in the past or else to focus completely on the present. Clinging to the past, either through indulging in happy memories or through feeling bitter about uncomfortable ones, is a refusal to accept the reality of my new situation. It refuses to recognize the 'painful-but-alive-now' moments and instead wallows in self-pity. The reverse is just as destructive: trying to shut my mind to what has happened is denying the significance of my marriage and pretending that it meant less to me than it actually did. With any form of denial, I am storing up trouble for myself, since feelings that are not recognized simply go into cold storage, waiting to be acknowledged.

The difficult thing to do is to live in both worlds simultaneously, and it is only this uncomfortable dialogue between now and then that can offer any prospect of transformation to my beleaguered self.

My raw visceral grief is reshaping how I see myself and forcing me to discover new ways of being in the world. It is this grief that gives an edge to my need to adapt. Unhappiness both purges the past and shapes the future, and it is this that will enable me to take on the best of what has happened while leaving behind the dross. For the Israelites in exile, writes Walter Brueggeman, hope always comes after grief.[2]

Shakespeare offers us the idea that where we have come from is a candle behind us, lighting the way ahead:

> *To-morrow, and to-morrow, and to-morrow,*
> *Creeps in this petty pace from day to day*
> *To the last syllable of recorded time,*
> *And all our yesterdays have lighted fools*
> *The way to dusty death.*
> MACBETH ACT V, SCENE 5, LINES 19–23

My dialogue between past and present is like a conversation between two people in which they start by shouting but gradually learn to listen and understand what each means to the other. Painful memories make uncomfortable companions. They chafe and rub against each other. Ultimately, though, God is the God of how life is, and there is a progression in the way things unfold. Events have consequences, and my history will first judge me and only then offer salvation. My marriage would never have collapsed if there had not been flaws endemic within it. The gap between the life I have dreamt of and the life I am living offers me either transformation or despair, and divorce will be the doorway to one or the other.

Divorce fractures my understanding of the past (are my wedding photos pictures of a happy day or a stark reminder of failed promises?) and thus shatters hope for the future. The future is shrouded when the past is removed: if I don't understand the past, I am not going to make sense of the future. Even so, it is my memories that teach me to understand the present and give me a platform from which to recognize how things will be in the future. It will be a different type of future from the one I had expected, but it is the things that don't fit with my previous expectations, or which are uncomfortable now, that will shape the person I am to become. I can insulate myself against some of the effects of my broken marriage but I can't afford to cut myself off from the person I was then. My identity as a once-married, now-divorced man is both the reason that I am suffering and the framework within which I will interpret the future. If I forget my marriage, then I am only half a man.

Dialogue with scripture

Memory and anticipation run together in a theological worldview. One provides the framework for interpreting the other: 'Remember your Creator in the days of your youth, before the days of troubles come' (Ecclesiastes 12:1). The Israelites were told to remember that they had been slaves in Egypt (Deuteronomy 5:15), and each year, at the Passover, they gathered to remember that just as God has liberated them in the past, so he would do again in the future. Zechariah remembered the holy covenant between God and his people (Luke 1:72) because it was only by understanding Israel's history that he would be able to make sense of the role to be played by his son, John the Baptist.

The actions of God are always new but they are cast in the moulds and images of old memories.[3] In other words, nothing that happens to us is ever lost because it becomes a part of the way that we understand and interpret the world. For example, David—once a shepherd and later a king—used the remembered image of a shepherd to describe God.

Old memories can be counterproductive, however. Jesus was constantly cautious about being categorized according to people's preconceptions about what the Messiah was going to do. He was unable to speak of himself as the Messiah until after Peter had acknowledged him as such; if he had laid claim to the title any earlier, his words and actions would have been slotted into already existing categories. He would then inevitably have been misunderstood— either written off as an imposter or lionized as the political Messiah for whom Israel had been waiting.

What Jesus did instead was to adopt and adapt Peter's acknowledgment of him as the Christ, in order to present himself as the suffering servant (Mark 8:27–31). He used people's categories of interpretation in order to subvert their expectations of him. Thus he used the past to understand the present and so to shape the future. He went to Jerusalem in order to root his actions in Israel's history and tradition. 'No prophet can die outside Jerusalem,' he reminded his disciples (Luke 13:33), and so it was there that he would be crucified. Even on the cross he used words from Israel's past (Psalm 22:1) to express his feelings of being abandoned; to lose sense of history is to lose the sense of possibility. No one standing by the cross would have realized the contribution that would be made to the history of the world by this bedraggled death on a poky hill just outside Jerusalem.

Christian doctrine both interprets and is interpreted by divorce. Eschatology is the study of the teachings in the Bible concerning the end times, the period of time covering the return of Christ and the events that follow. Divorce offers a parallel glimpse of eternal life: it offers the end of one way of being in the world and opens up the possibility of others. The idea of my divorced self living in two worlds, caught between the past and the future, is analogous to the idea of the Christian as a citizen of two countries—the earthly and the heavenly realm—being in the world but not of the world (John 15:19; 17:15–16). When Jesus talks about coming to bring not peace but a sword, he is talking about the breaking in of the kingdom of God (Matthew 10:34); it is one world overlapping with another.

Divorce offers its own version of this idea: it is a prism through which crucifixion and then eschatology can be understood. Each marks an ending—the ending of a marriage, the ending of Jesus' earthly ministry and the ending of the world. Endings and beginnings are templates through which the overlap between earthly and heavenly realms can be understood, and divorce teaches me how we live in the shadow land between the two.

My divorce is helping me to appreciate the subtle interaction between spirituality and physicality within the Christian faith; it is giving me the patience to understand the slow and gradual process of transformation as well as the earthy and physical nature of the resurrection. In *Darkness Visible*, William Golding uses two unlikely figures to explore the whole issue of redemption, salvation and transformation. What hope is there for Mr Pedigree, who is guilty of the worst crime possible within our society—being a child molester? What role is there for Matty, the horribly disfigured child, contemptible even to the touch of the molester turned reclusive adult? Mr Pedigree is a pederast, a sick and sad man, increasingly held in disgust by society and steadily sinking through less and less acceptable jobs. He starts as a teacher but then goes through jail and unemployment and furtive vagabondage round ancient and smelly town urinals—'sinking into a certain and sordid hell'. Matty is a child scarred and maimed, the left side of his face grotesque and skin-grafted, the right mobile and alive. His terrible burns were sustained during the Blitz:

The brightness on his left side is not an effect of light. The burn is even more visible on the left side of his head. All his hair is gone on that side, and on the other, shrivelled to peppercorn dots. His face is so swollen he could only glimpse where he is going through the merest of slits. It is perhaps something animal that is directing him away from the place where the world is being consumed.[4]

Within the book, Matty is the unlikely agent of redemption for Pedigree and rescues him from the grip of his 'internal rhythm' of sickness. It is the transfigured Matty to whom finally, at the point of death, Mr Pedigree appeals for release from the hell he feels doomed to endure.

Divorce is my grotesque and skin-grafted Matty. I am like Mr Pedigree, crying out for help in a situation that I cannot change, not realizing that my redemption lies within the very thing that I am hitting out against and want to move beyond. The unlikely agent of my redemption and transformation will be the destruction caused by the divorce.

Christianity constantly collapses endings and beginnings into each other. The cross is the central image of Christianity, and it is an indicator of the transformative power of rejection. In addition, the physical nature of the resurrection teaches me to trust to the completeness of my eventual transformation. Wright spells out how this might be. He defines some parameters for the way the early Christians understood the idea of the resurrection. He says that Jesus' resurrection appearances were an embodiment rather than simply a resuscitation of his old self. Jesus was a physical being, eating a meal with the marks of his crucifixion still visible. Wright uses the phrase 'transphysicality' to describe this—a body that is still robustly physical but also significantly different from the present one.[5] While the present physical body is not fully affirmed, it is not to be abandoned as it stands. It is to be transformed, changed from present humiliation to new glory (Philippians 3:21).[6]

The idea of a bodily resurrection draws a direct link between the temporal and the eternal, since what happens to me now is a part of the person I will become at the point of resurrection. Just as the resurrection body is similar to but different from the physical body, so also the resurrection experience is similar to but different from the life lived here on earth. The promise of resurrection is restoration and fulfilment, not avoidance and escape. This promise offers me the chance to make a friend of my past. Divorce is such a clear ending that a glimpse of life beyond a divorce is also a glimpse of eternal life.

As Wright says, history matters because human beings matter; human beings matter because creation matters; creation matters because the Creator matters.[7]

DIVORCE IS LIVING IN EXILE

How I understand my divorce will depend on the metaphors I choose to describe it. Metaphors are ways of seeing and understanding the world; they speak of one thing in terms of another as if they were the same thing. For example, Jesus is described metaphorically as the bread of life (John 6:48) or the light of the world (8:12). Christian believers are described as jars of clay (2 Corinthians 4:7) or as a temple (1 Corinthians 3:16). The temple image focuses on the transcendence of God and the pot focuses on his immanence. In other metaphors, the Bible uses the physical idea of journey as a way of describing the spiritual life of faith. In both Matthew and Mark, Jesus' ministry is represented by his journey from Galilee to Jerusalem: Galilee is seen as the sphere of revelation and redemption, and Jerusalem is seen as the place of rejection (though ultimately leading to resurrection).[8]

Metaphors shape an understanding of truth. The church will often prefer static images such as 'temple' or 'jars of clay' to images of 'journey' (Matthew 25:14) and 'movement', such as exile or exodus. However, the Old Testament offers me different metaphors of movement that I can use both to interpret my experiences and also to reimagine the future shape of my life. Walter Brueggeman sees in the Hebrew scriptures three great stories of God's people in different states of homelessness, or dispossession. He sees them as:

- Sojourners—Abraham, Isaac and Jacob—faithful folk on the way to a land whose name they didn't know.

- Wanderers in the wilderness with Moses and Aaron, where the people were at their most volatile and vulnerable.
- Exiles, displaced in Babylon, alienated from the place that gave them identity and security.[9]

In this book, I am bracketing these three images of movement ('sojourner', 'wanderer' and 'exile') under a collective understanding of 'exile' and 'exodus'. The exile is not simply a geographical fact but a theological decision;[10] it is a way of looking at the world through the eyes of God. What differentiates exodus from exile is that the exodus leads towards and the exile away from home. Exile literally means to leap out of something as if pushed, so the following characters serve as examples:

- Adam and Eve are in exile from the garden of Eden.
- Cain kills his brother and his punishment is to wander endlessly in exile across the earth.
- Noah is sent away in exile from the world he once knew.

The exodus is different. It is a journey with a mission, a journey of discovery. For example:

- Abram and Sarai go into exodus to the land promised to them by God.
- Moses leads the Israelites from Egypt into exodus so that they might find the promised land.

Exile has a sense of nostalgia; exodus has a sense of yearning. Both suggest the idea of longing—a sense of having left what is familiar and safe, and a searching for home.

My divorce has helped me to realize that this sense of yearning is a basic human emotion. It is the same sentiment expressed by Dorothy in *The Wizard of Oz*, wearing her ruby slippers and saying 'There's no place like home.' It is ET, in the 1980s Steven Spielberg film, wanting to 'phone home'. It is my feeling like a stranger among my own friends and family. In essence, divorce has made me aware of things that I knew but had not realized; it has made me aware of the existential situation, as it is and as it has always been. Ben Okri, the Nigerian writer, wrote that to be born is to come into the world with an inextinguishable sense of exile.[11]

The theme of 'leaving home to stay' reappears continually in films. *The Motorcycle Diaries* is the story of the young Che Guevara, in which he travels on a 5000-mile journey through the South American continent (his exile) and works out what matters most to him, seeing evidence of the injustices and separations that he will later fight against. *Finding Neverland* is the story of J.M. Barrie, the English playwright who wrote *Peter Pan*. Barrie's travels (his exile) are in his imagination, using playfulness as a counterpoint to tragedy. *Ray* deals with jazz musician Ray Charles' blindness (his exile), which gave him the acute sense of hearing that would under-pin his later music.

My divorce is an 'exile' that has ended up as an 'exodus'. It is a banishment from the security and happiness of a marriage, which has become a consciously chosen journey into an uncertain and indeterminate future. Wiesel described the 20th century as the age of the expatriate, the refugee, the stateless and the wanderer.[12] My being forced into exile has helped me to understand the exodus. I have become the nomad—the unsettled, roaming and restless traveller, symptomatic of contemporary living.

Scripture constantly cautions us against setting up a false and rosy picture of an idealized past. This helps me to avoid comparing my situation to the mythical ideal of a happy family: smiling couples and happy children simply reinforce my sense of isolation. (Women who have miscarried have talked to me of suffering from exactly the same feelings.) I can't unpick what has happened and revert to some earlier, more stable and happier part of our marriage. Neither can I jump forward, somersault the implications of what has happened and fully arrive and be at one with my new situation. Exile as a metaphor for being divorced steers me past the danger of idealizing a cultural mythology of a happy marriage. It also prevents me from being trapped by the idea that being in a relationship is a societal norm, which has been lost through divorce and will be returned to at some stage in the future.

Being in exile is more than simply a longing to return; it is a way of looking at the world—as an outsider putting things in perspective. Louise, who was married and pregnant at 16 but then divorced after 19 years of marriage, said, 'I think it has made me much more open to other people's experience, to people who have lived non-standard lives. It's humbling, and I *hope* it makes me more compassionate and less willing to judge.'

Claudia, whose husband left her after the birth of her first child, said the following:

I look at the kind of person I was in the relationship—quite sensitive, quite timid, quite shy, not terribly secure and needing somebody else to help me with my security. But actually I think that... I wouldn't be where I am now if I'd still been married to Mike, as a developed person with the understanding, empathy, professional development and personal development that I've got. So I'm a richer person as a result.

The image of exile and exodus represents the idea of transition and movement as a permanent state. Judah's infidelity towards God was a condition that existed from its earliest days as a nation. Through the entire history of the covenant, there never was a time of faithfulness (Jeremiah 4:1–4). Within scripture, there never was a time of stability when things were good enough as they were and did not need to change. An invisible norm of security and well-being exists only in people's minds. There is not and there never has been a safe space in which I can hide.

In the New Testament, the Bible uses the language of living exile: we are aliens and exiles with no permanent place, longing for home (Hebrews 11:13). This is the plight of us creatures in this post-resurrection, pre-parousia situation.[13] V. Bauman characterizes the self in postmodernity as either a vagabond or a tourist, the vagabond being a pilgrim without a destination, a nomad without an itinerary.[14] I feel as if I am a scrappy little tramp, wondering, wandering and waiting for what will emerge.

The use of exile as an image for my divorce allows me to focus on this immediate period without confronting 'hot button' issues such as the rights and wrongs of getting divorced in the first place, or of remarriage following a divorce. I can look at how exile-consciousness locates itself within the idea of liminality rather than in endings and beginnings. Liminality (which I look at later: see page 53) is a midpoint between two different ways of being in the world, where a person is no longer one and not yet fully the other.

The image of exile means that I can also focus on divorce as a loss of social identity rather than simply as a personal trauma: in the biblical account, exile was a collective experience for the Israelites and not one that was individually negotiated by each member of the community.

Exiled from the past

The history of the exile is as follows. After the reign of Solomon, the original nation of Israel split into northern and southern kingdoms —Israel and Judah. Assyria and Egypt were the two most powerful empires of the time, and Israel lay in the middle, relatively powerless and at the mercy of each of the superpowers. The influence of Assyria being on the wane, Egypt had first fought against but then allied with Assyria against the emerging and much larger threat of the Babylonian empire in the east. Between 609 and 605BC, Egypt took control of Judah as a part of the fight against Babylon. However, Babylon was expanding too rapidly to be contained.

The rest of the story is told in 2 Kings 24 and 25. During the reign of Jehoiakim, in 587BC, Jerusalem was captured and Judah was finally absorbed as a part of the Babylonian empire: the king of

Babylon exiled all the inhabitants of Jerusalem, burned the temple and tore down the walls of Jerusalem. King Nebuchadnezzar had invaded Judah three times, each time deporting kings and leaders of Judah into Babylonia and leaving the poorest and least powerful behind. Once in Babylon, the Jewish population were able to live in their own settlements and follow their own customs but they could not return to Jerusalem.

In 538BC, the Persian Cyrus II conquered Babylonia and allowed the Jews to return home, 50 years after the original sacking of Jerusalem. The Jews began the process of returning to the land of Israel and rebuilding Jerusalem and the temple. Ezra received official permission from the Persian authorities to return to Israel and take charge of the Jewish community. He found the Jewish social and religious life in Jerusalem in a mess. The law (Torah) was no longer observed and the walls of the city were in ruins (Ezra 10:18). Nehemiah reported, 'They said to me, "Those who survived the exile and are back in the province are in great trouble and disgrace. The wall of Jerusalem is broken down, and its gates have been burned with fire"' (Nehemiah 1:3).

The people were unhappy when they returned to Jerusalem (Isaiah 40:1–3) because there was no glorious kingdom of God established after the exile, as they had anticipated. The return from the exile was grindingly anticlimactic and took place over several generations. Isaiah talks of the cities being 'long devastated... devastated for generations' (61:4), which emphasizes the period (probably almost a hundred years) from when the first exiles returned home. The length of time it took for the returning people to get the rebuilding of the nation underway also disturbed the post-exilic prophet Haggai (see 1:4).

Divorce blends together Brueggeman's understanding of both exile and exodus. My exile leaves me feeling powerless and displaced. My exodus is a conscious transition from one thing to another. Exile consciousness is not simply a marking time, waiting for things to return to how they were before; the exodus led to 40 years in the wilderness. It is the framework of exodus, then, that is offered as a permanent template for how to understand God. The first of the Ten Commandments begins, 'I am the Lord your God, who brought you out of Egypt, out of the land of slavery' (Exodus 20:2). It might have been more impressive to say, 'I am God who created heaven and earth, time, space and all of reality itself.' Instead of this, God presents himself in reference to the exodus, which was just an individual event pertaining to only one nation in all of history. He did this because the exodus was relevant, verifiable and still a clear memory for the people to whom he was speaking.

While 'exodus' is presented in the Old Testament as a positive choice to journey, to move from one life to another, it is not true to say that 'exile' is presented as being simply what happens when things go wrong. The image of exile is one of a permanent semi-detachment. There is no idea of a comfortable status quo in which things will eventually settle down. That is 'a sharp and dangerous image that cuts across an ideology of continuity and well being... a yearning for equilibrium [that is] an idolatrous escape from reality'.[15]

Being in exile is a recurring process of discovery and self-realization. There is a continuous making of mistakes, a learning and relearning (engagement, disengagement and reengagement) among the central characters in the biblical narratives. Eve ate the fruit from the tree and then Cain killed Abel. God promised Abram the earth but Abram immediately panicked and told Pharaoh that Sarah was his sister (Genesis 12:13). Jacob cheated his brother Esau of his birthright, then fled to the east before coming back to face his brother and wrestle with God (Genesis 32). Joseph's brothers plotted against him and he was then sold as a slave in Egypt, where the family later joined him to escape the famine. Change is integral to the life of faith. Disjuncture and disequilibrium are repeated themes in scripture. Here are some further examples.

- The book of Acts is a sustained polemic on the need for the apostles to reframe their understanding of God. Peter needed to give up his commitment to dietary laws after his dream in the city of Joppa (11:4–10). He changed his mind over circumcision on the basis that it was forcing Gentiles to follow Jewish customs (Galatians 2:14).

- Hosea married an adulterous wife, knowing that he would be betrayed by her (1:2).
- Habakkuk worshipped God despite the fact that his cattle died and his crops failed (3:17–18).
- Job worshipped God because the collapse of his personal circumstances and the lack of any reasonable explanation for what had happened led him to accept that the God who made the Pleiades and Orion is beyond standard human explanations (38:31).

There remains a constant ebb and flow in the relationship between God and Israel, due to the inscrutable way in which God is constantly prepared to pick up on the consequences of Israel's choices, even when they do not accord with his will for a situation, and draw the people back into a covenant relationship. An example of this comes when the people of Israel decide that they want to have a king, to be like other countries—someone who will judge and rule them, go out before them in battle and fight for them (1 Samuel 8:4–22). They have already got God on their side but they want more. The prophet Samuel highlights the oppressive way in which kings behave (v. 10) and God makes it clear that their desire to have a king is a rejection of him (v. 7). Nevertheless, a king is what they want and a king is what they get. The implication of this decision will be fully realized only with the destruction of Jerusalem and the exile to Babylon in 587BC.

Exile is both judgment (*krisis*) and opportunity (*kairos*). In New Testament Greek, *kairos* means a right or opportune moment, a time that is right for change; *krisis* is a moment of judgment. My exile is a 'judgment' in so far as the marriage has ended but it is also an 'opportunity' in that it gives me the context to rethink my place within society. If exile is seen entirely as judgment rather than opportunity, then healing and wholeness can come only through reversion to how things were previously—and I can never move on. If exile is seen entirely as opportunity rather than judgment, then I risk being glib about the whole process—and I will never learn from my mistakes.

In terms of the whole society, also, exile is both judgment and opportunity. I look at this issue further in the chapter headed 'The family', where I argue that the prevalence of divorce has created multiple different types of family configurations—and that the church can no longer support family life simply on the basis of defending the nuclear family structure.

Exile is not a static image, with a strong, stable motherland waiting somewhere to welcome people home. For the Judeans, the exile was not simply a matter of leaving Jerusalem and soon returning to the very same city. The nation went into captivity for 70 years. Some people went into exile, never to return. For those who did go back, Jerusalem was a different city from the place they had left: it was a city in ruins, a land under Persian rule, with less than full freedom (Nehemiah 9:36–37). The people who rebuilt the temple were different from the people who were there at its destruction.

There is no road map, either, for what happens or what needs to be done in order to survive once a marriage has ended and the divorce has gone through. I am having to relearn how to relate to those closest to me: relationships of some years' standing are on a knife edge as I feel my way towards making sense of what has happened. The rationale of exile is subversive and transforming, looking for different ways of understanding the world. So the idea of being in 'exile' offers me images of change, movement and growth that are truer to my experience than more static categories of interpretation. As Walter Brueggeman says of Jeremiah, 'The poetic practice in Jeremiah is to seek for a language that is passionate, dangerous and imaginative… as much concerned with the invitation of imagination as with the practice of ethics.'[16]

Exile in the present

The exile in Babylon was both punishment and preparation for the Judeans. The collapse of Jerusalem is an appropriate image for me to use in relation to divorce as it provides the etymology of a disaster and a template for how to deal with any calamity. However, Jeremiah and Isaiah represent two different approaches to coping with the disaster. Whereas Isaiah urged repentance as a way of saving Jerusalem (Isaiah 30:15), Jeremiah wanted the residents of the city to accept the reality of exile and the destruction of their city, and then to seek the peace and prosperity of the place to which God had sent them (Jeremiah 29). One part of me is Isaiah, still believing that I can do something to rescue the situation. The other part of me is Jeremiah, because it is easier to accept and adjust to a new situation than to challenge and change it.

Jeremiah does not romanticize the idea of going into exile: Judah still had to face the anguish and pain caused by the realities of the situation. For Jeremiah, however, exile is not simply a punishment, a difficult time of testing before being allowed to return. It is a permanent condition. Home is no more a place of security, stability, refuge, nurturing and safety than exile is a site of danger, insecurity, instability, threat and anxiety. This is equally true of my situation. The reality is that I live my life in a state of permanent transition, and divorce has simply made me more aware of this fact.

Jeremiah highlights two reasons for what happened in Jerusalem and each of them provides insights into my own situation. The first reason was autonomy. Judah had grown to think of itself as self-sufficient, the arbiter of what was right and wrong with no need for recourse to God. The temple had come to mirror back to the nation a sense of its own importance rather than a glimpse of the sovereignty of God. The covenant promise had been choked by the social reality of the temple authorities' collusion with the king: they fed back to him what he wanted to hear about his behaviour and failed to confront him with the claims of a living God. In Brueggeman's words,

'The sin of Judah is an effort at theological, political, historical autonomy, the nullification of Yaweh's governance of public life.'[17]

People get married thinking that it will last for ever, but a marriage is no more inherently durable than was the temple for the Israelites. Claudia, whom I mentioned earlier, told me how her marriage imploded after the birth of the first child. She said:

I think one of the strengths of a relationship that starts in your late teens/early twenties is that you grow up together, and you're making friends, and we had a lot of friends who we saw regularly. Then they got married and then we got married—we were both 26. So the relationship had been going on eight or nine years. And what happened was that some of our closest friends' marriages broke up. We could have gone through our wedding album and removed photograph after photograph. It was incredibly destabilizing and really upsetting. With our closest friends it happened once Catherine had been born, so Catherine was a baby and we had this huge trauma. We were in our second home by this time. But I thought that everything between us was fine and we were stable. Simon meanwhile had set up on his own in business as a solicitor and I was left at home with quite a difficult baby.

I know what it is. You give the male all the attention he needs and everything's fine, but when there's somebody else who's getting the attention, you're on a loser. You're covered in sour milk, sick and everything else; you're a complete shambles; you haven't slept… and you reflect and think, could it ever have been easy?

So I've mulled this through, and what's deeply distressing is that somebody you thought you knew, really knew… suddenly becomes a different person. It wasn't just the fact that that happened to me, because I was able to rationalize it and say, well, I'm 31, I'm very attractive, I've got my whole life ahead of me. If this person no longer loves me, then providing he provides for my child and me, that's fine, that's the way it has to be. That was the approach I tried to take. But anyway, he just walked out. He came home one evening and said, 'I'm leaving.' He couldn't cope with himself, so he left—and Catherine was only a year old.

Claudia's marriage collapsed because the arrival of the baby and the lifestyle implications of having a child pushed her and her husband apart rather than drawing them together. The Old Testament narrative takes this cause-and-effect one step further, with God being described as actually dismantling the previously unquestioned world of Jerusalem (Jeremiah 15) when it no longer fulfilled the purpose for which it had been created. The consequence of this was the exile, and the result of the exile was a new way of understanding God's place within the world. The temple had previously been seen as the place where heaven and earth met, the one place where sacrifices could be offered (Deuteronomy 12). Its destruction and the subsequent exile of the Israelites in Babylon tore apart the assumption that God needed to be worshipped in that one place. The exile separated an understanding of God from one particular socially constructed habit of worship.

This teaches me that God does not owe us his Holy Spirit, and he is prepared to draw back from something that no longer fulfils the purpose for which it was created. Doctrinal correctness is no guarantee of good behaviour and a Christian marriage can't claim God's protection by right, simply because the vows were made in his name. Simon, in the example given above, was asking too much of his marriage in wanting his wife and child to mutate around his new career and the subsequent process of what he saw as self-discovery. He got tired of trying to make it work and so he walked out.

In William Golding's novel *The Spire*,[18] Dean Jocelin of the Cathedral Church of the Virgin Mary has set himself and his building crew an impossible task: to add a 400-foot stone spire to the cathedral, despite the fact that the building has no foundation and cannot support such a structure. Obsessed by a vision, Jocelin persists and drives those around him through financial problems, internal dissent, fire, plague and death. The building of the spire becomes more important than the vision of God that it is intended to represent. In the same way, the Jerusalem temple also became more important than the purpose for which it was created.

The second reason highlighted by Jeremiah for the fall of Jerusalem was independence. The Jerusalem temple was no longer the embodiment of the covenant promise; instead it had become a distortion of itself, exercising a form of social control over the people in Israel. The eternal purposes of God had become too connected with the ideology of the temple. Yahweh had become too closely tied into a social system of values and policies and conduct, and so he chose to withdraw. Brueggeman comments, 'The temple and its royal liturgy are exposed as tools of social control... the Temple is shown to be not an embodiment of transcendence but simply an arena for social manipulation.'[19]

Sarah and I both behaved independently. We were accountable and answerable to each other but in public terms there was little more than that. Our actions with each other became entirely self-referencing: we became the arbiters of our own choices, and these choices then took the whole situation beyond our control. Just as in Jerusalem, once things started to happen, a train of events was set in place that would lead inexorably towards a conclusion. Our marriage was made by contract rather than by covenant. A contract is an agreement between two or more people to do (or not to do) something. It consists of an offer, an acceptance and receipt of consideration by each party to the contract. A contract is good in business but bad in personal relationships: it can make people seem as if they are categorized by what they do rather than by who they are, and, ultimately, marriage becomes a disposable commodity.

In Claudia's story, it transpired that Simon left her because there was another woman involved:

When it happened, my GP said, 'There's another woman.' She said, 'Most men can't survive by themselves; they have to have that other person there.' And there was, although I didn't know for nine months. What happened was that somebody rang me and said, 'We've got to tell you this...' In fact, he'd been having an affair—while I had a very tiny baby and was struggling with this baby.

In a covenantal relationship, obligations cannot be fully specified in advance: I promise faithfulness whatever may come of it. A covenant commitment to a person is open-ended and not time-limited. There is no honourable exit: it is 'for better or worse, for richer or poorer, in sickness and in health, as long as we both shall live'. For Sarah and me, the reality has proved sadly different.

DIVORCE AND BEREAVEMENT

When Sarah and I were on our honeymoon, we said to each other that it would be preferable to be bereaved than divorced from each other. She actually said that she would prefer to see me knocked down by a car and killed than for the two of us to have to go through a divorce together. It was a passionate statement, though sadly, for us, not borne out in practice. Divorce has similarities with bereavement, although, in the immediate aftermath, it is more scrambled, confusing and difficult to deal with than bereavement.

If Sarah had died, the end of my marriage would have been unmistakable and non-negotiable. She would have been mourned and missed; life without her would have been difficult and horrible but, once the body had been buried, the situation would have been clear and resolved. By contrast, my marriage has died but there is still a walking, talking, living body. Emotionally, the situation is complex. It is not just a question of mourning. I am also thrown into the challenge of reassessing our time together: what did and what does it all mean? How do I make sense of old wedding photos?

With bereavement, the history of the relationship becomes enshrined; the meaning and significance of events becomes clear. The story of the past is intact, even if the ending was unexpected. The dead person and the survivor's relationship with them becomes sanctified and set in stone. When a marriage ends through separation, however, the past takes on a very different hue. Even the bits that seemed good at the time take on a different complexion in the light of later events. When a marriage ends through the death of a partner, there is a fixed point in time at which life as a widow(er) begins: I was a married person but now I am no longer. There is no middle ground. Now that my marriage has ended through divorce, there is an interminable middle ground. This is a liminal period in my life.

DIVORCE IS A LIMINAL PERIOD

'Liminality'—meaning a period of transition when a person is caught between two different situations—is derived from the Latin word *limen*, which means 'threshold'—that is, the bottom part of a doorway that must be crossed when entering a building. It has the sense of going from one place to another. My story in this book does not start until after my marriage has finished, and this post-divorce state is an intermediate, liminal period. I feel neither married nor single. I have not fully let go of one way of looking at the world and taken up another. The past is not quite over and the present is not quite here. Technically and legally, I am no longer married, but emotionally and practically I cannot think of myself as anything else. I am betwixt and between, work in progress, neither fully one person nor yet another, a long way from being able to put my experiences into a wider context. I can't go back but I am not ready to move on. I am on the edge of one way of understanding my place in the world and on the cusp of another.

Liminality is a wilderness situation, away from one place but not yet in another. The image of wilderness suggests emptiness and aloneness, a place of tough struggles, complete failures and decisive encounters, but it is also a place for hopeful new beginnings. It is the time between the collapse of one set of plans and the emergence of another, a time characterized by openness, ambiguity and un-certainty. The threshold is a place of both pain and knowledge. It gives me the chance to rethink how I want to relate to the world.

My life is at once empty and full: I have little to do but a lot to think about. I am the person 'poor in spirit'—'blessed' in the Beatitudes (Matthew 5:3) because the realization of my own needs and vulnerabilities teaches me how to appreciate others: awareness of emptiness brings compassion. I pray for people; what else have I got left to do? The ethic of liminality is not perfection but consciousness; it is awareness, not behaviour, that is reshaping my sense of self. I am able to change who I am in relationship to society; I am not trapped in spaces that no longer belong to me. The jagged edges of fear caused by my divorce teach me to re-engage with what others expect of me and what I want of myself.

One of my reasons for using the concept of liminality to look at my divorce is that I am consciously avoiding dealing with the beginning and ending of the process. The beginning would be the question of how to avoid getting divorced, while the ending would be the question, 'Once divorced, would it be wrong to get married again?'

Churches can handle the issue of remarriage clumsily because, often, the church will not be alerted to the issue until it presents itself as a real possibility. Louise (quoted earlier in this chapter) tells her story of how the issue was tackled in her own church:

Our vicar felt he should have a discussion about divorce because some people were asking. So there was a meeting at the neighbourhood centre, and I hated it so much. He just let people talk. (It was two or three months after [Princess] Diana was killed.) He presented some of the biblical texts on divorce—which Steve [Louise's new husband-to-be] and I had talked about, and I think they're vile. I may not be a very good Christian, but I hate them. The vicar did go through the scriptures and it was very clear that [remarriage] is not just frowned upon, but it's wrong. So that's fairly hard to take but, OK, we're all sinners. But then the discussion was opened and instead of talking about divorce or scripture, it was diverted into a discussion about whether Prince Charles should marry Camilla. It went on for an hour, and it became a discussion about the hierarchy and the class system and I just thought, 'What is going on?' and the vicar couldn't seem to stop them. I couldn't speak, I was spitting mad. I wasn't going to say anything. I just didn't know how to…

Divorce is presented by the church either as something to be avoided at all costs or else something to be got through as quickly as possible. Within Christian literature, the ideal of the family is such an integral part of the Christian tradition that divorce needs to command a commensurate weight of censure. Divorce—the thing to be avoided at all costs—becomes an adult version of the bogeyman in children's stories: the child is warned that the bogeyman will come if he does not eat his pudding, and the adult is warned that a divorce is the fallout if he does not make his marriage work. Divorce can also be presented as the ultimate challenge of Christian credibility—the 'valley of the shadow of death' in which the believer is comforted by the shepherd's rod and staff (Psalm 23). Treating divorce as a liminal period avoids these apocalyptic treatments of the subject.

The end of the divorce process is also well covered within the Christian literature on the subject. At one extreme, David Robertson writes about how the lessons learnt through his divorce re-equipped and re-energized him for his second marriage.[20] At the other extreme, Wenham and Heth write that remarriage after divorce is always adultery and should be seen as such.[21] The idea of liminality also allows me to avoid these Christian 'hot potatoes'.

There are two reasons why this book actively avoids the subject of remarriage. The first is that to focus on remarriage would be unfair to those who are divorced and still alone. The book would become a version of the oft-repeated Christian narrative of the believer whose faith is tested but who remains true to his belief, in which an 'I-never-believed-I-could-be-so-happy-again' relationship is seen as the evidence of God's faithfulness. The fallacy in this logic is that some people, after a divorce, do marry again (and again and again); others do not, either by choice or because they are unable to meet someone suitable. I do not wish to leave those people who are divorced and still alone, through no choice of their own, feeling disempowered and dispirited.

The second reason that this book does not look at remarriage is that an argument in favour would come closer than I am comfortable with to legitimating divorce, and an argument against would alienate some of the people best able to benefit from what I have written. Remarriage is a subject in its own right, and I want this book to be about divorce.

Treating my divorce as a liminal period allows me to avoid analysing the breakdown of my marriage. Jerusalem is already abandoned and in ruins, as is my marriage. Oscar Wilde wrote in *The Importance of Being Earnest* that the truth is rarely 'pure' and never 'simple'.[22] There are reasons but not explanations for why my marriage has broken down and ended in divorce. I am not sure that even I can fully explain what they are and, even if I were to parade all the events up and down in front of you, you would still not have a clear picture of how or why I ended up in this predicament. There is a Chinese proverb that says, 'If you want a definition of water, do not ask a fish.' By extension, no one can assume that I know the full set of reasons for the end of my marriage.

Therefore, this book is not written as a forensic examination of the reasons for my divorce, and it is not concerned with establishing who was right and who was wrong. The companion question to 'Why did it happen?' is 'Who is to blame?' and I have no interest in this question. Whatever the answer, it does not alter the reality in which I find myself: the marriage has finished and I am on my own. My immediate future is in exile and my need is simply to survive. I once described my feelings to a friend with the image of being punched in the stomach by a stranger while walking down the street. It is not my responsibility to analyse the punch; it is my responsibility to recover from it. I am a casualty but I am not a victim of circumstances. My task is to decide what the next step is, which way to turn, and then to act, trusting in God's faithfulness.

When the envelope containing the decree absolute drops through the letterbox, a divorce is legally endorsed. The death of the marriage is acknowledged by nothing more than a certificate. The moment is both an end and a beginning: it is the final seal on the process of separation, begun months or even years before, and it is the official, legal acknowledgment of life as a newly single person. For me, the moment itself was an inconspicuous and unemotional piece of formality at the end of a drawn-out and highly emotional drama.

The process that led towards my decree absolute felt like an interminable middle ground. Some people may travel through it relatively quickly, but for me it seemed a slow, seemingly endless grind. It was messy and full of uncertainty. Jane, who was left by her husband, describes it thus:

The journey was a rollercoaster ride through peaks of real hope, when my husband gave tentative indications that he might want to return and restore the marriage, and troughs of confusion and despair when those words turned out, apparently, to be empty.

For a failing marriage, there is never a single 'moment of death'. People talk of various significant moments along the way: the acknowledgment that the marriage has descended into a tangle of misery and misunderstanding; the initial discovery of a partner's unfaithfulness; a partner moving out of the marital home; the decision to begin divorce proceedings. Sometimes these moments are seen to be significant only with hindsight. Even the realization or decision that a point of no return has been reached—that I am no longer in a marriage and that I am facing the future alone—may not be a single moment in time but a gradual process of recognition.

Liminality deals with a loss of social identity

The people who survived the exile had lost three significant markers of their relationship with God: the hope of a messiah, the temple and the promised land. Previously, God had channelled national blessing through the house of David, but now the Davidic king was in a Babylonian prison. Previously, the Israelites had brought their sacrifices to the temple, but now the temple lay in ruins and sacrifices could not be offered. Previously, the land had been the clear evidence of God's favour, but now it was no longer in their hands. Judea had become a backwater province of the Babylonian empire.

This break between empirical circumstances and an understanding of God happened distinctively and dramatically three times in Israel's history. Adam and Eve were banished from the garden of Eden, Noah saw the earth flooded, and Isaiah saw Israel in exile. In a parallel piece of social stripping, my divorce tears away the significant points of my public persona and forces me into different ways of relating to the world. I can no longer draw security from marriage as the social expression of my Christian faith. In the New Testament, Jesus gives a parallel challenge to the Jews. The inbreaking of the kingdom of God means that they can no longer draw security from the fact that they are sons of Abraham. What they see as privilege, he sees as promise, meaning that if they do not obey his commands then they are, in effect, illegitimate children (John 8:31–41).

Divorce is a social transition as well as a personal tragedy. When I tell people what has happened to me, they read themselves into my story and imagine how they would cope if the same thing happened to them. This is because the account I give to others of my own experiences draws on language and imagery common to everyone: my personal story of the experience is, at the same time, a socially constructed explanation. Macintyre describes social life as enacted narrative.[23] The idea that there is a socially constructed self is a key theme to the book—looking at transitions. I can see that there are basic similarities between my getting divorced and other transition points in my life. When I went to primary school, I did not want my mother to hug me at the school gates. When I went to secondary school, I no longer wanted to be met from school. When I went to university, I no longer had time to ring home. There is a period of adjustment needed after any significant life event: the process of deconstruction and reconstruction is endemic to any period of change. In other words, there is nothing unique about the coping skills required by divorce.

The biblical story of salvation repeatedly shakes our understanding of God free from too rigid a view of our socially constructed self. God is both transcendent and holy, and also incarnated and earthy. Transcendence can't be contained and incarnation can't be constrained through conformity to one particular way of being in the world. No situation is beyond redemption but that does not mean that God will protect people from themselves and the responsibility for the life choices they have made. Previously, my marriage was expressive of my belief in God. Now, instead of this, my divorce has become the public presentation of the fragmentation in my life. The idea of exile gives me a theological framework to express this experience.

EPILEPSY

At the same time as dealing with divorce, I have had to learn how to cope with epilepsy. It is an uncomfortable piece of symmetry: each becomes a mirror to the other, the internal medical collapse matching the external social fragmentation. Epilepsy reinforces what is becoming the central theological lesson for me during this period— the loneliness and the detachment of the person in exile. I made the following recording in my journal:

I am told by the doctors that I have got a special condition whereby I can suddenly and sharply lose the ability to make the basic connections necessary to working out what is going on around me. I maintain my awareness of a situation but lose any sense of balance or perspective. I know that there are people around me but I don't know who they are; I can't bring their faces into focus and so friends or family or colleagues—whoever I am with at the time—become briefly, in my mind, nothing other than unfathomable shapes and noises. My memory bank is wiped out and I lose all the most basic information about who I am, where I am, who other people are and what it was that I was doing.

Each episode, it seems, is only a snapshot of a few moments but it still leaves me needing to reformulate what I do and what I do not know. I have to reconnect basic sensory information with my own knowledge base. I have to reconstruct ideas as thoughts. I have to relearn different actions as a habit.

A whiplash of light leaves me feeling giddy, sick and confused. I have a slipping sensation of separateness. It is like the flashlight of a camera exploding in front of my eyes—the brightness pushes everything else out of focus. I am momentarily quite unaware of what I had been doing. It does not matter whether I had been talking, running, walking, sitting, listening or watching. Whatever it was, I am no longer a part of it. Everything becomes suspended and separate. It is like looking at an old television where the picture is blurred and the voices are fuzzy. I lose my understanding without losing my consciousness. It is a form of non-conscious consciousness where I am aware only of my detachment and remoteness from everything that is happening around me.

The sensation is like slipping into a nirvana; it is not always unpleasant. I am jogging and am caught by a giddy, sick sensation at the base of my throat; then I plunge into nothingness. I am still jogging but I do not know the time or the place of where I am. I find myself caught on the edge of conversations, suddenly quite unaware of who anyone is, what they are doing and what they are saying to me… who indeed I am and what I am doing. Faces are frozen; images are suspended; any conversation or activity hangs in the air. I am completely absent in sensation—my mind pulled away from people, places and activities. Image and information become disconnected from each other so that familiar patterns become strange and presupposing. I stand in my own home and have to guess which door leads to the bedroom. I am in the bath, startled that I am lying naked, covered only by soapy warm water. I have lost the ability to turn information into knowledge and so I can't make sense of anything that I see.

Suddenly, I am parachuted back into consciousness. It is a quick and sudden, bewildered rush of impressions—where I am; who I am. What has been happening? Is there something that I should have said? Is there something that I should have done? Is there some place that I should have been? I am only gradually able to reassociate which image goes with which picture. Everything is sharp and crisp and loud. The whole process has taken seconds rather than minutes and no one has even noticed what has happened. It has all gone on in my head. It is a surprise to me that everyone else has not been through the same rocketing turbulence. They seem to be carrying on as if nothing untoward had happened.

This internal disintegration can happen once or twice a week. I try to protect myself from harm. I won't drive a car and I won't ride a bicycle—the car because it might hurt other people and the bike because it might hurt me. I came off my bicycle once, due to an absence, and came to with a woman screaming about what she had seen happen. What could I do? I did not know what had happened that had made her scream. I stood up and walked away. I am the 'there, not there' man. Epilepsy means that I can phase out in the middle of a conversation and be back before someone has finished what they are saying. The process is scary, strange and sometimes even wonderful for me, but inconsequential and unremarkable for anyone else. They don't know it has happened.

My illness has left me a stranger to myself. Now I am always looking in from outside, brittle in my crumbling confidence. It does mean that, once or twice in a week, I can be looking at everything completely afresh as if for the first time—any cloak of familiarity no longer hides anger, kindness, humour or tiredness in people. I can see everything in primary colours.

PROVIDENCE

Christian teaching that stresses the importance of discovering and being faithful to God's plan for our lives can instil in people a subtle but strong sense of failure if things do not work out well. People can end up feeling as if the wrong choices have been made. For example, if God has one single storyline planned for my life, then the fact of divorce is simply failure and offers no opportunity for redemption. I work with Stella, a teenage girl who has unexpectedly become pregnant. Her immediate comment to me was that now this had happened, she would be 'no use for the kingdom of heaven'. I want to reassure her that God's providence is not simply and only a series of right and wrong options; his plan for our lives is not a predetermined route that we have to follow. I tell her that God's providence is more like knots in a tree than a motorway through the heartland. God can offer direction but still allow people a freedom to follow different routes. Isaiah explains, 'Although the Lord gives you the bread of adversity and the water of affliction, your teachers will be hidden no more; with your own eyes you will see them. Whether you turn to the right or to the left, your ears will hear a voice behind you, saying, "This is the way; walk in it"' (Isaiah 30:20–21).

Christians can be tempted to conceive their lives in terms of 'givens' from which they dare not deviate instead of gifts that they can incorporate into the evolving story of their lives. Wells draws parallels between a situation (such as mine), an understanding of providence and what happens when actors improvise a drama.[24] There is an element of choice and self-authorship in the way a story develops. Christians should learn the skills of an improvising actor —when to block a suggestion made by another actor and when to accept it by incorporating it into the evolving story. When a suggestion is blocked, it is because the new line seems to lead away from the previously agreed plot outline. When a suggestion is accepted, it is seen as an opportunity to enrich the drama without losing the story's thread. R. Williams puts it like this: 'My vocation is not a given set of tasks to be completed. It is to be the person I have it within me to become. The act of creation can be seen as quite simply this—the vocation of things to be themselves, distinctive, spare and strange.'[25]

Imagine a vase that has been cracked, broken and then mended with gold paste. The article that emerges from the debris and damage will, unexpectedly, be more beautiful than it was before. It will be the same vase but different, because the cracks have been incorporated into its make-up. This vase is an image in my mind of my hopes for the future. I want my divorce to be the gold paste that mends the cracks in my life. Divorce means that I am going to have a very different life from the one I might have otherwise expected, but then, I don't think that there ever was a single, divinely ordained script set in stone for how I should live my life? This is a theological reality that I have understood but never fully acknowledged before.

LONELINESS

Divorce has left me vulnerable. At the same time, it is an invitation to repattern my relationships, with God, with other people and with myself; I need to find new ways to understand myself, in order to relate to other people. Up to this point, I have lived my life in three-year, student-sized chunks and I have always been able to experiment with different ways of being in the world. I have always had multiple groups and communities to which I feel an affinity and I have been able to choose how to present myself in different ways according to the context.

Constant options, flexibility in work and commercially driven lifestyles mean endless choices with socially fluid structures of identity. I have always learnt to adjust the way I relate to the world whenever a significant and unexpected change occurs, and I am now realizing that divorce has not created a new or destroyed an old 'me'. It has helped me to understand the way I have always been. A loneliness has always been there within me but I have rarely, if ever, acknowledged it. Now that I am divorced and on my own again, loneliness is the terror of living with complete freedom. I no longer have to consider another person in the choices I make or the identities I shape.

The feelings of being lonely, unknown and isolated in an anonymous crowd are endemic to the human condition. My divorce has simply made me more aware of them. R. Williams writes that Christians seem to treat the subject of loneliness with a consistent lack of seriousness and with a painful lack of imagination and sympathy,[26] while Henri Nouwen points out that the word 'loneliness' best expresses our immediate experience and therefore most fittingly enables us to understand our brokenness.[27]

Singing the Lord's song in a strange land

Henri Nouwen writes that to live a spiritual life we must first find the courage to enter the desert of our loneliness.[28] My desert is by the 'rivers of Babylon', learning how to 'sing the Lord's song in a foreign land' (Psalm 137:1, 4, NRSV). Like the Israelites, I need to come to terms with what has happened in the past in order to begin to make sense of what might happen in the future. There is no security for me in creating false absolutes, either writing off my marriage as if it had been all bad or idealizing it as if it had been all wonderful. Each caricature is a distortion of the facts; inevitably my marriage was neither as good nor as bad as I might imagine it to have been.

I am on my own, wondering how to make sense of the fragmented set of events that I have been through. Learning how to 'sing the Lord's song' is a strange, sad and eerie experience. It is the challenge to anyone feeling excluded, shunned or shut out of what is going on. It is also the institutional question that needs to be asked by the church in order to understand its role in society. We are all 'aliens and strangers in the world' (1 Peter 2:11).

The answer to this question, according to Brueggeman, does not come through thoughts and hard work but through faith and imagination: '[We should] ask not whether it is realistic or practical or viable but whether it is imaginable... poetic imagination is the last way left in which to challenge and conflict the dominant reality.'[29]

Brueggeman outlines the challenge facing the exiled Israelites (which is a parallel to the situation facing me). At one extreme, there was a danger in distancing themselves from the memories of their time in Jerusalem. At the other, there was a danger in hiding amid waves of nostalgia for a period that was past. The way in which the Israelites interpreted their situation in exile was irrevocably tied to how they understood their past in Jerusalem. Their grief at being in exile emerged because they *did* remember their previous life in Jerusalem. These happy-sad memories then became the seedbed for their imagination as they sought to 'sing the Lord's song'.

Cutting themselves off from their past life in Jerusalem would have meant making an absolute of the present and becoming absorbed into the Assyrian culture, losing any understanding they had had of themselves as the people of God. It was only the memories of their time in Jerusalem that reminded them of who they were and so prevented the erosion of their identity: 'Psalm 137 is a passionate resolve not to be assimilated... [it is a] polemical theological imagination that guards against cultural assimilation.'[30]

It would have been equally as destructive, however, for the Israelites to cling to the memories of their past life in Jerusalem and refuse to engage with the reality of their new life in Babylon. As we have already seen, Jeremiah cautioned them against this and challenged them to seek the peace and prosperity of the city where they were living in exile (29:7). The Church has to deal with the same challenge—steering a correct path between either over-identification with or detachment from the surrounding society. Lesslie Newbigin explains:

One can speak of the path which the church must take as lying between two dangers. The first danger is that the church may so conform its life and teaching to the culture that it no longer functions as the bearer of God's judgment and promise. It becomes simply the guardian and guarantor of the culture and fails to challenge it. The other danger is that the language and the life-style of the church should be such that they make no contact with the culture and become the language and life-style of a ghetto.[31]

The task is to remember well. The Israelites were so angry that they wanted to take the children of the Babylonians and dash their heads against the rocks (Psalm 137:9). They were grieving at the destruction of Jerusalem and trying to reimagine themselves back into a relationship with God. Anger and grief are natural parts of that recovery process. Yet, at the same time, there is a natural progression of events. The way in which the Israelites dealt with their social and theological displacement shaped a refreshed and reinvigorated understanding of God that would eventually be expressed through a new covenant (Jeremiah 31:31), and ultimately through the coming of Christ. The challenge to the Israelites, as to me, was neither to deny nor to take refuge from past memories, but simply to remember well.

When we remember well, our hurt, anger and indignation become transformative, subversive, imaginative memories.[32] If I am able to accept, own and understand my past, the present is full of possibility. The experience of being divorced means that transition and change have become a template for my life. Freedom, for me, comes through the idea that if things were different in the past, then they can be different again in the future. I am left badly bruised but with a passion for the possible. I become like the servant awaiting the return of his master (Matthew 24:46), or like Hamlet recognizing the hand of providence:

There's a divinity that shapes our ends,
Rough-hew them how we will…
There is a special providence in the fall of a sparrow. If it be now,
'tis not to come; if it be not to come, it will be now; if it be not now,
yet it will come—the readiness is all.[33]

✦

THEOLOGICAL CRAVINGS

In this chapter I consider the dangers of looking for oversimplified answers from my Christian faith. Divorce has ended my marriage but it has not finished me as a person. It will shape and shame me but it will not decide me. I am not going to be trapped by what has taken place. In order to avoid the trap, however, I need theology to be a redemptive and transformative discipline. This does not mean that there is a deep, dark and delicious theological panacea that will solve all my problems by giving me easy, catch-all, one-stop answers, thus easing me smoothly through every difficulty. There is no theological placebo that will make it seem as if bad things never happened. The crucified Jesus is not an easy answer to anyone's troubles. The cross engages with the reality of sin, so it never pretends that sin is not present and powerful in the world. Theology offers me salvation through, rather than protection from, suffering.

I crave clarity and certainty as an antidote to my divorced condition, and the Christian constituency can feed these theological cravings (as I call them) by offering me the lure of a theological ideal in order to eliminate doubt and uncertainty. Ultimately, however, this craving for all-defining and absolute answers can only be destructive because, in looking for too much from theology, I expect too much of myself in return. I want to do my best, but grace can be squeezed out by duty, and so my desire for theology to provide clear, crisp and comprehensive answers makes me feel worse than ever. As Pattison writes, the responsibility for change and forgiveness lies with those who have had to bear most in the first place and may have the fewest inner resources for effecting reconciliation.[1]

I have considered my theological cravings under three 'headings': guilt, sin and forgiveness. None of these offer me the full explanation I am looking for; the truth is more subtle and nuanced than the theological banner headline might suggest. They can provide part of an explanation for my situation but they put unnecessary pressure on me if I expect any more of them.

Guilt provides a partial analysis of my situation, because I feel shame as well as guilt at what has happened. My divorce is not a situation that can be repaired or undone, so my sense of failure is as much to do with myself as a person as it is to do with specific things that I have or have not done. Pattison comments, 'The assumption of guilt is that I am in control of my situation, able to repent and decide on a different course of action (normal). A sense of shame may often accompany a sense of guilt… Guilt implies responsibility and the possibility of action through the mechanism of repentance and reparation.' [2]

Sin also provides a partial explanation: it offers analysis without solution. Sin may be followed by repentance but repentance will not undivorce me. Finally, forgiveness provides a partial explanation because it offers solution without resolution. Forgiveness will salve but not solve the situation I am in. Again, I can forgive for all I am worth but I will still be divorced.

GROWING INTO AN UNDERSTANDING

The decree absolute ended the marriage but it did not end the emotional and practical consequences of the divorce. A situation is defined by the way it is understood—diagnosis is everything—so I have choices about how I make sense of and respond to the events. If I see myself as the victim, then I feel hard done by. If I see myself as the instigator, then I feel guilty. If the two are mixed together (as in my situation), there will be a struggle to comprehend everything. I need to understand in order to survive, and, as Joey Fagan says in the 1991 film *The Commitments*, 'once you have a start, the rest is inevitable'.

There are two sorts of understanding: one is spoken and the

other is felt. The first is the understanding of arrangements of meetings and plans, of rational thoughts and conversations. It proceeds smoothly enough, like walking along a pavement. The second is the understanding of shame, grief and fear, of feelings, aspirations, hopes and dreams. These emotions are like shifting sands and stormy currents; they include glimpses of beauty and terror, which do not translate easily into words. A spoken understanding can be described and acted upon; a felt understanding must be absorbed and grown into, and the latter is what I am now feeling my way towards.

Ideas are the tools I need to get at this truth. I want my Christian faith to be like a surgeon's knife cutting into the reality of my experience. Scripture offers illumination and insight: it is a two-edged sword, picking apart the 'soul and spirit, joints and marrow' (Hebrews 4:12). In theory, 'theology, far from being a source of certainty, is an interpretative discipline, which seeks to make sense of human experience on the basis of a belief in God'.[3] In practice, though, no sooner do I start looking to theology for help than I start feeling wrongfooted. I am beginning from a default position because I am divorced but I feel doubly disadvantaged with my craving for theological absolutes—and the Christian constituency appears to be feeding my habit.

For the best of all possible motives, Christians can take an ideal picture of the 'perfect' believer as a tacit norm, which leaves people feeling that it is their fault if they have not lived up to this ideal. Theological cravings assume a 'redeemed and sanctified' view of human nature and underestimate the reality of sin. This makes huge assumptions of those of us within the church, who are essentially a group of ever-fallible human beings, struggling with our faith, constantly failing and in need of grace and forgiveness. Theological cravings look for triumphant Christian living. The emphasis is more on 'I can do all things through him who strengthens me' (Philippians 4:13, NRSV) and less on 'I do not do what I want, but I do the very thing I hate' (Romans 7:15, NRSV). This positive spin on Christian living is due to an entirely understandable eagerness to demonstrate the benefits of faith and to model something to others that looks wholesome and attractive.

What this means, though, is that I am embarrassed to admit failure. Theological craving presents a 'could be' as a 'should be'. This is particularly daunting for me: we all want to do our best but at the moment I am struggling to do the basic minimum needed to keep myself together and my faith intact. Divorce involves more than a simple sequence of confession, repentance and forgiveness. God can forgive me but I still have to live out the emotional and practical consequences of what has happened.

Tillich characterizes theological cravings as a 'pathological' need for 'security', 'certainty' and 'perfection'. He says that such a need is instinctive and becomes destructive only when the possibility of 'insecurity', 'uncertainty' and 'imperfection' is denied.[4] The danger is that, having absorbed an implicit but unobtainable theological standard, I am tempted to grab at certainty substitutes to fill the emotional gap.

I could clutch at 'security', for example, by hiding behind other people—go out and date someone else and take comfort in another relationship. I am coming very close to this, going for lengthy dinners with different women, lasting long into the night. In reality, it is a form of emotional trespassing, with me looking for comfort and intimacy in new friendships. There is always a certain frisson to a new relationship that goes a long way towards dispelling my post-divorce lethargy (I never realized that being unhappy was so tiring!). Andy, my Huddersfield-supporting lodger, tells me that when I go out with people for these long dinners and late-night conversations, I should 'talk but not touch'! (He is right: going out with someone on the rebound never works.) I could grab at 'certainty' by hiding behind what I say and being definitive and defensive in how I interpret what has happened: I could create a narrative in which it was either all of my fault or none of my fault. Then I could ease the need for moral 'perfection' by hiding behind a lazy guilt. Guilt shows a lack of responsibility in that I just wallow around in my own feelings, which frees me from any need to engage constructively with the demise of my marriage.

Raw and authentic Christianity does not offer 'security', 'certainty' and ' moral perfection' as a universal remedy to the situation I am in. Christian truths are not cough sweets to make me feel better about myself.

SHAME RATHER THAN GUILT

Guilt alone does not resonate with my situation: I am feeling deeply ashamed to be divorced. Yet the church's structure of confession and repentance appear only to be addressing the guilt. Guilt is the feeling that I have broken an external code of conduct. Shame is the feeling that I have let myself down. As Pattison explains, 'The modern shame- rather than guilt-directed individual self is more concerned with inward perceptions about the success of the self in living up to its own ideals about itself than it is about the transgression of clear, externally defined rules and standards.'[5]

Pattison suggests that a sense of shame may often accompany a sense of guilt,[6] and this is true of me: I feel guilt as well as shame; it is both-and rather than either-or. As I have already mentioned, however, my story has been that the church sees shame and reads guilt. The church offers me 'a system of confession and penitence fuelled by shame but articulated as guilt. This is infinitely self-perpetuating. It is unable to foster either integration or forgiveness because often it fails properly to address either shame or guilt. While guilty people need forgiveness, shamed people need a sense of valued self'.[7] The more my shame is treated as guilt, the worse I become.

In conversation with an older woman, I told her of my shame in being divorced. She told me that she also feels ashamed to have married children but no grandchildren. Henri Nouwen agrees with

Pattison that there is a shift from a guilt culture to a shame culture in our society.[8] Louise (mentioned earlier) echoes this in her description of how she felt following the end of her marriage:

A friend came round and took me to a doctor because I couldn't stop crying. I had this little baby who wouldn't have understood what was going on, and it was really important to me that she didn't pick up all the distress. So I just felt 'I've got to hold myself together', and I didn't have any family near me. The strange thing was, I felt such a lot of shame and stigma. I couldn't even do things like go to the post office and say 'I need my single parent's allowance' or whatever it was you could claim. I didn't do that for months because I couldn't face that this had happened to me. It just completely destroys your self-esteem and your confidence, everything. I really had to pull myself up, and I used to tell myself… I used to say things like, 'Well, it could be so much worse—I could be married to Saddam Hussein. I could be a starving African. Just look at what I've got.' And in fact Amy says to me now, 'Mum, you're so good at thinking about what's positive in everything.' But I don't know whether that's in my genes or whether it's learnt behaviour.

Let me remind you of Pattison's comment: 'The assumption of guilt is that I am in control of my situation, able to repent and decide on a different course of action.' I am not in control, however: repentance hasn't mended the marriage and forgiveness has not removed the social stripping of divorce. I feel guilty because I have broken the moral and ethical code of the church. I feel ashamed because I have not lived out my marriage vows: I have fallen short. I have failed to live up to my ideal self. I have put my hand to something that did not work out and now never will. Inevitably, I am left feeling that a part of this failure stems from my own inadequacies, such as having made the wrong choice of marriage partner in the first place or having made mistakes within the relationship. I feel the weight of the words 'failed marriage'. I have invested my very self in something that has now collapsed. Ultimately I feel that I have let God down.

Susan, another of the people I spoke with in the course of writing this book, articulated this perception most keenly when she said, 'I felt guilty because my intellect told me that the gospel was the truth and that somehow I was letting God down, and I couldn't let myself go to church, I suppose for about three years.' I have not stopped going to church but I have stopped singing hymns. I feel that it is easier to stay silent than to praise God on an empty stomach. My failure has led to a loss of confidence in my own judgment.

Guilt needs redemption and shame needs transformation—and both lie within the incarnation. When the incarnation is seen as a direct follow-on from the creation, then Jesus' coming to earth is a further expression of God's love rather than simply his response to the fall of humankind. Even if Adam had not sinned, Jesus would still have been incarnated. This reading of the incarnation throws the emphasis on to the original goodness of God (in the creation narrative, 'God saw that it was good': Genesis 1:18) and on the incarnation as an act of transformation. It makes creation not simply a one-off act of origination but a continual and ongoing engagement of God with the world. When, on the other hand, the incarnation is seen as God's rescue plan, triggered by human sinfulness, the emphasis is focused on humanity's original sin (as summarized in Romans 3:23) and on the incarnation as an act of redemption.

I need both redeeming and transforming. The redemption saves me from the consequences of sin; the transformation shapes me, ready for the new life that will be mine. The theological promise is that the redeemed and transformed believer is invited to participate in the ongoing work of God's revelation, which will culminate in a new heaven and a new earth (Revelation 21).

SIN

In scripture, sin is connected with repentance and responsibility rather than with failure. There is a perverse comfort in the idea that the situation is my fault and I am being punished for it: if I can convince myself that divorce is sinful, then I can feel good about feeling bad! This explains how sin can be a 'theological craving'. Guilt leaves me feeling a failure; divorce is loss plus failure, but even a sense of failure does not lessen my responsibility. Jamieson, Mcintosh and Thompson all describe us as being called at the point of failure.[9] What they mean is that a realization of our need becomes a point of growth. A sense of failure is the flipside to an understanding of freedom. It requires a 100 per cent recognition of responsibility for what is my part in the problem and a 100 per cent freedom from responsibility for what is not my part.

Guilt leaves me feeling sinful. There are two distant echoes from my childhood that give me an ease and familiarity with the idea of sin. The first comes from long afternoons spent on a beach in Norfolk, bored, with nothing to do, waiting for parents who would sit by a beach hut and read. My mother used to tell me that if I was bored, it was my own fault. The second comes from my father, who repeated the idea that 'life is unfair' like a mantra, wanting us as children not to take anything for granted. My understanding of sin emerged out of this early-formed recognition that things were not as they could be. My father was telling me that I had a responsibility to look after myself, in the same way that my mother was saying that I had a responsibility to amuse myself. As the new kid on the divorced block, I don't want people saying '"Peace, peace"… when there is no peace' (Jeremiah 6:14). Sin reassures me because it helps me to know where I stand. It gives me a responsibility for my situation.

King Hezekiah had to learn that his sin affected the whole of the rest of the country (Isaiah 36:7). This is the the same lesson that I now have to learn: sin is a public and not a private affair. God would not protect the people of Judah from themselves: he was prepared to let the consequences of their actions work themselves out. In the Old Testament, sin was not seen as an action distinct from its consequences; for Judah, it was the beginning of the chain of events that would lead eventually to ruin. The sin and its penalty were spoken of as if they were the same thing.

The consequences of sin always reach much further than the immediate protagonists. This insight helps me to understand why the failure of my marriage has had repercussions beyond my immediate family and myself, why so many people have been drawn into the process of disintegration. Marriage is not a wholly private affair; it is also a social arrangement, deliberately made in the context of a community. The effects of divorce cannot be kept wholly private between the two protagonists because the marriage covenant is made in the context of the wider church and society. John Donne wrote, 'Each man's death diminishes me', and my divorce diminishes my family, friends and church community. After the collapse of a marriage, people get drawn into the chaos that ensues. I do not have a monopoly on pain and I am not the only person involved in the process. The end of my marriage is not something that just happened to me; it is something that affected my family, my friends and the wider community of which I am a part.

All sin is an offence against God rather than just against another person. In legal terms, this means that sin is the equivalent of a 'criminal' rather than 'civil' offence. If sin was judged by the equivalent of 'civil' law, and the person I had wronged was not present, then there would be no obligation on me to do anything as recompense. In effect, the fact that Sarah and I are no longer seeing each other would get me off the hook. However, sin is judged by the equivalent of 'criminal' law, and this means that there is a duty of response on everyone. No one makes a conscious choice to fall short of the glory of God (Romans 3:23) but there is a deliberate choice involved in deciding how to respond to the shortfall. It is sin and responsibility, rather than sin and fault, that are the natural companions in scripture. Fault-finding is all about blaming myself or other people. Responsibility means recognizing my part in what has happened and then responding accordingly. This idea of individual responsibility is a healthier construct than personal blame.

The dignity of repentance is found in the fact that I can begin the process of distancing myself from the sequence of events and reestablishing myself as an actively thinking, deciding, feeling person: I am no longer defined entirely by past events. I may be someone who has been divorced but I am not just a divorced person. I may be a victim but I am not a loser. Steve Griffiths describes himself as being refined but not defined by the death of his wife, and draws an analogy between his grief at the time and the story of Jacob's wrestling (Genesis 32:22–32).[10] My temptation is also to define myself by my divorce—to use the term 'divorced' as a shorthand phrase for 'self'. There is a security in feeling miserable: it means that I am required simply to cope and nothing more is expected of me. To look beyond that misery to a reshaped future feels unnerving.

Grace and sin

Using the idea of sin to help me to understand my divorce helps me also to understand God better. This is because the way I understand sin determines how I will understand grace: the greater my understanding of one, the stronger will be my sense of the other. The more I can draw strength from an understanding of grace, the more I will be looking to God to see what he is going to do and the less I will try to fix things for myself. In the words of Isaiah, if I am able to take my strength from tranquillity, quietness and trust, then 'whether [I] turn to the right or to the left, [I] will hear a voice behind [me], saying, "This is the way; walk in it"' (Isaiah 30:15, 21).

In the stillness of radical Christianity, I know that I cannot judge, because I cannot fool myself into a sense of superior righteousness. This stillness of faith is a patient waiting, full of hope—a gesture of confidence in the meaningfulness of reality. The holiness of this

God, of things as they are, is inevitable and indivisible. His mercy lies beyond, not this side of, judgment. Apart from the grace of Christ, those who sow trouble reap it later (Job 4:8). The history of my divorce is the judgment on my marriage but also its redemption.

Revolutionary stillness is a way of doing nothing; it is what the Bible calls 'repentance'. The word has become so weighed down with emotional feelings of guilt that the point of repentance can be lost. Repentance is the recognition that the process of healing depends on deeper, more actual and urgent forces than anything I can muster on my own. The belief that I can do nothing constructive to help the situation is not an indication that nothing constructive is being done—and therein lies the heart of the Christian story of redemption.

I wrote the following in my journal:

The idea of doing nothing to achieve something appears illogical. The natural assumption would be that I should at least try to do something. If ever I was in trouble at school, I would scuffle around trying to hide what I had done. This would then be replaced by a sinking sensation of dread when I realized that I had been caught. Divorce and the realization of God's grace are like the same situation, but in reverse. It is when the ensuing feeling is one of relief at being found out, known (1 Corinthians 13:12) and accepted.

Accepting redemption is easier said than done. In a similar way to forgiveness, which I look at later in this chapter, grace is counterintuitive. There was a period, before the divorce was finalized, when the idea that there was nothing more I could do to improve the situation seemed unconscionable. I couldn't help thinking there must be something that would make a difference—one more meal, one more drink, one more present (an expensive black jade necklace). The idea of accepting that everything had now passed beyond my control felt like madness. I blamed myself and got locked into a cycle of justification, pleading, hoping and worrying. There was no pride or balance or reasoned judgment in what I did. There was just a blind belief that if I threw myself at the situation, something would change. I would be tender, angry, romantic and sad; I would be anything Sarah wanted me to be. Inevitably, a hope that there must be something I could do hardened into a blind belief that there were things that I *must* do. Gradually, as, one by one, these initiatives failed to work, the realization came that there was nothing I could do.

I was like King Hezekiah who, when faced with the destruction of Jerusalem, refused to recognize that the situation had passed beyond his control and that he could not sort things out for himself. God offered redemption but Hezekiah wanted a solution. God mirrored back to Hezekiah the consequence of his sins. Hezekiah wanted to privatize sin and make it his responsibility to cope. Isaiah's fundamental challenge to Hezekiah was that the whole body politic was corrupt and that there was no such thing as a private sin. Faced with the mounting crisis of the Assyrian invasion, the king made an alliance with Egypt to protect his land (Isaiah 20). For Isaiah, this alliance was both theologically corrupt and politically naïve. It was theologically corrupt because Hezekiah had caused the situation in the first place and now he was taking the entire responsibility on his shoulders to sort it out. He was trying to script God out of any possible solution. To try to deal with the situation by making an alliance with Egypt was to address the symptoms of his country's collapse while ignoring the causes. The alliance was politically naïve because Egypt was nowhere near strong enough to stand up to the Assyrians. The situation within my marriage went beyond my control a long time ago but, just like Hezekiah faced with the Assyrians, it took me a long time to recognize it. Repentance and faith can be more difficult to maintain than strength and determination because they mean giving up keeping my nerve, and recognizing that there is nothing for me to do.

Punishment

The fact that divorce is a sin does not mean that I am being punished for it. Suffering is not a punishment for bad behaviour, just as wealth and prosperity are not a reward for good behaviour. Jesus unpicked the idea of a religious meritocracy in which people earn blessings or are punished for wrongdoing, saying that God 'causes his sun to rise on the evil and the good, and sends rain on the righteous and the unrighteous' (Matthew 5:45). In other words, God treats all people indiscriminately. Both the good and the evil suffer. God is God. His ways are mysterious and we cannot know them. Jesus describes a new reality underpinned by God's grace, in which it is not what people do that is significant but what God has done for them. We are saved by God's faithfulness to us rather than our faithfulness to him.

The idea that I am being punished for my divorce ties the actions of God into my behaviour. This is the flipside of the mistake that the Israelites made in connection with the temple, when they assumed that God's blessing was theirs by right. It was actually Yahweh who dismantled Jerusalem: he is pictured in Jeremiah 6:6 as leading the fight against the city. God gives freely but owes nothing. He can act in an unprescribed and unexpected manner, and does not *have* to do anything at all. He does not owe the Holy Spirit to human beings.[11]

Brueggeman writes, 'God's free, unfettered, massive holiness… is a constructive force making new life possible.'[12] Divorce is a critical standing ground for imagination. That torn space in my heart is a holy place, giving a glimpse of the sovereignty of God. On the basis that God's purposes in the world may make use of Babylon (Jeremiah 25:9, 27:6), Assyria (Isaiah 7:18–20) or Persia (Isaiah 45:1), there is no reason why my divorce should not be a point of unfolding learning and grace for me.

In the case of divorce, where there is a dramatic collapse of circumstances, the disparity between theological ideal and social reality is keenly felt. I draw a distinction in this between what is 'usual' and what is 'normal'. 'Usual' is a repeated sequence of events, a regularity of practice. 'Normal' is just who I am. My divorce is unusual—it breaks a pattern of living and a way of being in the world—but that does not make me abnormal. Normality is a particular social expression of myself, appropriate to specific circumstances. I was not born preformed; my identity is also socially developed and constructed. Being made 'in the image of God' (Genesis 1:26–27) can indicate a way of relating to the world as much as an essential, inner, core part of being human. My situation in the world has caved in but it is how I make sense of all this, as much as what has actually gone on, that will shape how I emerge from the experience. If I conflate these two ideas of what is normal and what is usual, it puts extra pressure on me. I am left feeling that not only is there something wrong with the situation but there is also something wrong with me; not only have I broken the social ideal of a happy fulfilled marriage but I have also failed to live up to God's expectations for my life.

The early origins of what became known as 'feminist' theology highlight the danger for the church of being tied too closely to socially constructed views of 'normality' as a framework for theological interpretation. Feminist theology challenged the tendency for biblical hermeneutics to be shaped by the prevailing hegemony (that is, assumed ways of interpreting the world). It offered other paradigms of interpretation to Christian religious traditions largely shaped by men. For example, it drew attention to the fact that God can be seen as 'Mother'. The Lord is portrayed in the Bible as a nursing mother (Isaiah 66:13), a midwife (Psalm 22:9–10) and a female homemaker (Psalm 123:2). Jesus' encounter with Mary in Luke 10:38–42 can be interpreted as an indication that women should prefer studying theology to a preoccupation with domestic chores.[13] If Jesus' choice of twelve male (Jewish) disciples signifies that females should not be leaders in the church, then consistency suggests equally that Gentiles should not be leaders in the church.[14]

It is no comfort to me to refer back to an accepted norm, because it only serves to reiterate how my circumstances have changed. Divorce prevents me from drawing security from the idea that my marriage is a social expression and outworking of my Christian belief, but I am no less a child of God because my marriage has ended. In theological terms, God reveals himself through our socially constructed selves. There is an inevitable tension because God's freedom cannot be restrained by his accessibility. My divorce has pulled apart who I am in the world from how I understand God.

'The attempt to make Jesus conform to our understanding of things cannot help but domesticate and tame the wildness of God we worship as Christians,' says Hauerwass.[15]

The danger of the normality myth is that it encourages my desire for a safe space to return to rather than a reconstituted future to look forward to. I am left floundering, clutching at an ideology of order and well-being but without either the tools to achieve it or the wit to know how. All my conventional markers for orthodox Christian behaviour have disappeared with my divorce. My new situation now contradicts theological ideals of marriage. I have lost the focal point of marriage as a way of shaping how I see myself, so my structured world disintegrates. I no longer have a normal routine to my day: there is no order, no regularity and no routine to what I do. My accepted, acceptable and usual way of life vanishes, and this means a loss of certainty, confidence and security in how I understand myself and how I see my position within the world. I no longer draw strength from other people's respect; I am too frightened at what they might say.

Storms pass; everything collapses but not everything disappears. God is not in the earthquake or in the thunder but in the still, small voice of calm that comes afterwards (1 Kings 19:12). Divorce is awful in the way it pulls apart my way of being in the world but, apart from the scale of the disruption, it is not unique in the way it forces a readjustment of habits and expectations. Any transition, thwarted ambition or disappointed dream will do something similar and will require the same process of deconstruction and reconstruction in the way I might relate to the world. A network of meaning collapses and a new situation of faith and engagement emerges. It is not the breakdown of my marriage that brutalizes my sense of self; it is the way I am taught to understand and then interpret the experience. The challenge, as Pattison says, is that the church talks dirty, but can it actually cleanse and heal? [16]

FORGIVENESS

The idea of forgiveness tells me what I have to do but not how to do it. The Bible is clear about the need for me to forgive both Sarah and myself for what has happened: Jesus said, 'You can't get forgiveness from God… without also forgiving others. If you refuse to do your part, you cut yourself off from God's part' (Matthew 6:14, THE MESSAGE). It is not explicit, however, about exactly what this forgiveness entails.

Forgiveness is not a once-off 'now it has happened' moment in time. It is a journey. Today I might feel forgiving but tomorrow I will feel angry and hurt all over again. The idea of forgiveness needs to be properly nuanced in order to be understood: it is important to me to avoid creating a set of tighter expectations than are actually intended in scripture, which would put unnecessary pressure on me. Forgiveness can appear counter-intuitive. Nothing is less obvious than forgiveness[17] but, at the same time, nothing is more necessary.

There are two caricatures of forgiveness, both of which make me feel inadequate and dispirited because both are unrealistic and expect too much of me. The first caricature is the idea that I have to 'forgive and forget'. This feels like a refusal to engage with the reality of the situation, and it turns forgiveness into condoning the offence. It means blocking out or pretending that I do not mind what has happened. Feigned indifference is not forgiveness, however; it is simply an avoidance of the issue and hence, ultimately, nothing more than ignorance. Volf's understanding of forgiveness is earthier than this. He suggests that memory and forgiveness run close together. It is remembering what has been done that allows for forgiveness: 'To forgive is to blame not to punish… to name the wrongdoing and condemn it… the gift is not counting the wrong doing against them.'[18]

The second caricature runs forgiveness and reconciliation together, implying that they should be immediate and simultaneous. I can forgive in the sense of wanting what is best and right for Sarah's future. I can wish her well without any traces of bitterness or recrimination. Yet, if I saw her coming towards me, I might still want to hide and hope that she had not noticed me. In time this may change but, for now, forgiveness comes first and reconciliation might follow. Forgiveness is the intention; the possibility of reconciliation is an eventual outcome. The two do not have to happen simultaneously.

The idea that reconciliation should be an immediate, automatic and integral part of forgiveness is theological pressure at its most demanding, wanting the ideal to be a baseline for a standard norm of behaviour. Forgiveness is a gradual process and not a single moment in time; it is a journey towards wholeness—what Mackintosh calls voyages of anguish.[19] At times, I have wondered whether Sarah and I might be able to meet for lunch and have conversations as if we were friends rather than lovers. I have imagined different scenarios, with neither of us needing to take sides and everything being managed with decorum. The reality is that even considering this as an idea leaves me caught in the trap of wanting an ideal scenario at the same time as needing to reconcile myself to an actual situation.

Timetabled reconciliation is unrealistic. Anger is a form of dignity and feeling angry is my way of teaching myself that I deserve more than what I am experiencing at the moment. A total lack of anger would mean that I had internalized what had happened, accepting it as my due. Anger that lingers too long, however, becomes bitterness, and then I am thrown back again on to the need to forgive. Genuine forgiveness, in the sense of my wishing Sarah well for the future, does not require us to sit across the table from each other in restaurants and pretend that nothing has happened.

Claudia said this of the struggle she had to forgive her husband:

It always happened in church, in moments of silent prayer. I used to really think this through. I used to think it would be such a weakness in me to forgive him. People even used to say to me that he had been so appalling that it would be weak and pathetic for me to forgive. But then I went on a church weekend where the speaker talked about the ability to stand on the edge of a cliff with this stone—a millstone—and throw it into the sea, and until you can do that, you'll never be free yourself… I just remember crying and crying, and I came away from that weekend… I don't even have to talk to him about it or be 'big hugs and kisses and friends'—but it's something that happens inside me. It's for me.

There is a social script that wants me coping and able to manage. In that script, experiences are commodified, controlled, understood and moved on from. In our 'stuff happens' society, you have to just, well… 'move on'. At the moment, however, I am neither ready nor willing to do this. I need my theology to be raw, real and authentic. Forgiveness is intentional rather than emotive—it is not a single moment in time.

H. Williams writes, 'Theological truth is the truth of God's relationship with man and it is the fruit not of learning but of experience. In this sense, all theology, properly so called is written in blood.' [20] Divorce is too debilitating an experience to be parcelled out as a part of a learning experience. I have not grown through divorce. I have shrivelled and become a lesser man. At times I feel neither sad nor glad that it has happened. It has simply become a part of who I am. There are plenty of words for someone struggling or finding things difficult. When it comes to an inability to cope with the rubric of day-to-day living, the language jumps to emotive terms such as 'breakdown'. I am breaking down but I am not actually having a breakdown. I prefer the term 'meltdown' as being the most expressive of my situation.

I look elsewhere at the temptations either to demonize or to glamorize my history—at how each extreme offers nothing more than a short-term coping strategy. If I glamorize my marriage, then I feel nostalgic and I blame myself. If I demonize my marriage, then I feel bitter and I blame other people. Forgiveness will enable me to make a friend of, or at least accommodate myself to, what now must become my past. The relationship must have had cracks, otherwise it would not have collapsed, but the memories do not need to be all bad.

Forgiveness is a gift that I give both to myself and to Sarah. Receiving forgiveness is dependent on repentance but giving forgiveness is not. There are no terms involved in giving a gift. It is not a negotiation in which Sarah has to accept the conditions on offer. Forgiveness is a gift that we give to ourselves, since non-forgiveness comes from a lack of hope; it is a sullen resignation to the idea that things will not change. We can be chained by the idea that events will repeat themselves. In my weekly assembly at a local primary school, I asked the children why they thought it might be important to forgive people. A 10-year-old child shot his hand up. 'Please, sir,' he gasped, 'if you don't forgive you are frightened that it will all happen again.' Archbishop Desmond Tutu said of the work of the Truth and Reconciliation Committee in South Africa:

To forgive is not just to be altruistic. It is the best form of self-interest. It is also a process that does not exclude hatred and anger. These emotions are all part of being human. You should never hate yourself for hating others who do terrible things: the depth of your love is shown by the extent of your anger.[21]

Volf writes that forgiveness is also within the very nature of our beings. He writes that we should imagine our lives as a piece of music. We have heard this music played by a virtuoso and would like to play it well ourselves but, try as we might, we fail. The process of being able to play our music beautifully can start with our being willing to forgive.[22] Forgiveness is at the very heart of God's character.

Ultimately, the whipcrack sharpness of the need to forgive leaves me with no room for sentimentality. The choice to forgive or not to forgive is ultimately a choice between life and death; it is the choice between a slow disintegration into bitterness and self-recrimination or a reaching out towards a new beginning. This is what Isaiah offered to King Hezekiah. Isaiah writes as a poet rather than as a philosopher or historian: he uses words to paint extremes, either of ultimate peace, harmony and fulfilment or of complete destruction and chaos. Isaiah paints pictures with words. He writes, in beautifully crafted poetic language, vivid images of the best and worst things that could happen to Jerusalem as a consequence of Hezekiah's actions. If the king repents and turns to God, then all will go well. There will be 'no more gloom for those who were in distress'; the people in darkness will see a great light (Isaiah 9:1–2). 'The wolf will live with the lamb… the infant will play near the hole of the cobra' (11:6, 8). If Hezekiah does not repent, then things will collapse: destruction and chaos are inevitable. In such cases, 'the grass is withered; the vegetation is gone and nothing green is left' (15:6). Forgiveness is not an optional extra.

✝

THE FAMILY

The commonness of divorce within the UK has had a twofold effect. The first is to put pressure on the nuclear structure of family living and the second is to create multiple different types of family configurations. There is one strand of thinking that laments the former and focuses on the immediate threat to the traditional nuclear family; there is another strand of thinking that welcomes the latter and focuses on the emergence of different types of family structures. The first line of thought tends to be associated with a conservative and reactionary worldview, wanting to uphold tradition and order. The second line of thought tends to be associated with a more libertarian worldview, wanting to promote the individual's right to different styles of living.

My interest is in drawing the two together, blending theological orthodoxy with social diversity and seeing how best the church can promote a vision for family living against the background of the increasing normalization of divorce. My argument in this chapter is that we should not, out of a well-intentioned desire to support the nuclear family structure, underestimate the value of the energy within newly constituted stepfamilies. These can end up as a form of extended family that mirrors some of the patterns in other societies and even examples given in scripture. As Thatcher comments, 'There should be no contradiction in advocating marriage and honouring the best intentions of post married people who chose to form new families.'[1]

IS DIVORCE BEING MADE A SCAPEGOAT
FOR CHANGING PATTERNS OF FAMILY LIVING?

As Mr 'Now-I-am-divorced', I am a part of a wider social picture. Marriages in the UK appear distinctively fragile. The United Kingdom has the highest divorce rate in Europe—almost twice the European Community average in 1993.[2] No individual choice is isolated and unaffected by others, so the wider social context to the increasing levels of divorce in the United Kingdom is part and parcel of the situation in which I find myself.

As I chew my way through other people's food and sympathy, I am left wondering at the nature of their reactions to me when I tell them of my experience. The reality of my situation is that some people who were close friends to us both now treat me with politeness rather than warmth. It is difficult to know how to act or what to feel in response. They are not malicious, angry or ill-intentioned towards me; more often than not, they are confused. Their responses to my situation are often more about themselves and their feelings rather than about me and mine. They start the conversation by talking in extremes, and then they quickly come over all embarrassed, saying that they do not know what to say. They tell me what they think about my divorce ('How terrible!') long before they ask me for my opinion. Then they seem disappointed if I do not reply in similar vivid language and if, instead, I steer the conversation on to safe ground and discuss mundane topics, such as what I've done that day.

Other people's responses are an integral part of my making sense of the situation. Their confusion fuels my desire for the church to provide people with a theologically informed social script, so that those whose marriage has ended can be helped through the process of recovery.

The conversations people have with me become opportunities for them to rehearse back to themselves what they see as society's and the church's expectations of marriage. The danger in this is that in simply re-presenting their own thinking, they are not engaging with the reality of my situation. For example, the more idealized their view of the family, the more extreme the criticism they offer of divorce. Nothing is achieved by their comparing my fragmented reality to a 'perfect' family, because it is a best-to-worst comparison. A good family life is excellent and my divorce is awful, but the two situations do not need to be set off against each other for these facts to be established. I often feel as if I am a mirror, reflecting back to people the unease that they feel about shifting patterns of family life.

There is an important place for social disapproval. People's opprobrium can serve as social glue, helping to maintain the institutions on which society depends. In his essay *On Liberty* (1859), John Stuart Mill spoke of the value of 'social disapprobation'. If people were not disapproving, it would mean that they did not care. I would not want someone to be anything other than surprised or disappointed to find out that I am divorced. Any other type of reaction would mean that divorce had become so regular as to be unexceptional. Without 'social disapprobation', divorce can become a self-fulfilling prophecy: if it is anticipated, it becomes more likely to happen.

My failed marriage is an example of a wider social malaise. Scapegoating is a way for us to replay back to ourselves what we consider to be important: we reinforce our sense of belonging together by arbitrarily identifying someone or something else as an enemy or threat. The question I want to ask here is whether the phenomenon of divorce is being made a scapegoat for the breakdown in the nuclear family unit, and whether the reactions that I get from people are an indication of a society in transition, ill at ease with itself.

According to John and Olive Drane, there are at least seven distinctive types of family structure and domestic arrangements in Western culture today.[3] According to Hayman, there are around 72 different forms of family within the UK.[4] If divorce is treated as a scapegoat for the breakdown of nuclear family structures, then this wider reshaping of family living is ignored.

In scripture, the scapegoat was a goat that was driven off into the wilderness as part of the ceremony of Yom Kippur, the Day of Atonement (Leviticus 16:8–26). Two goats were sacrificed to atone for the sins of the Jewish people. One was killed in the temple, the other sent out to wander in the wilderness, symbolically bearing the sins of the Israelites. In the New Testament, Jesus was the archetypical scapegoat. He absorbed the ire of the Jewish leaders wanting to defend the legitimacy of the temple and, in so doing, redeemed people through his suffering.

Contemporary scapegoating is when someone or something is blamed for another person's misfortunes, which can then become a way of distracting attention from the real causes. The scapegoat is seen as the reason why things are not right; it creates cohesion and unanimity in the wider community. My suggestion is that divorce has become an easy scapegoat for a church wanting to promote the sanctity of marriage. If something can be labelled as the cause of the problem, then that can become the focus of attention and we are freed from the uncomfortable need to acknowledge our own responsibility for the changing shape of family life.

The dvastating nature of divorce makes it a perfect candidate to be a scapegoat for marriage breakdowns. Mol suggests that divorce can create more stress than one-off, life-threatening traumas such as road accidents, the murder of a loved one or physical assault. He suggests that people whose worst experience was a life event such as marital discord had, on average, more symptoms of post-traumatic stress disorder than those whose worst experience was a physical accident.[5] In an address at the Mothers' Union in Westminster to mark the International Year of the Family, Jane Williams compared the effects of unfaithfulness and divorce in this country with the ravages of war and Aids on family life around the world.[6]

At the same time, other research suggests a different way of looking at the same issue: a broken home is always a reconstituted family. 'The breakdown of one set of relationships is not leading to the death of the family but to its reorganization.'[7]

Research by Neale, Flowerdew and Sanders suggests that children of divorced parents are less willing to be labelled as 'trauma survivors' than adults might be ready to label them as such. They followed 60 young people aged eight to eighteen for four years after their parents had divorced, interviewing them at the beginning and end of the study. The research suggests that young people today are far less likely than previous generations to see their parents' divorce as a tragedy that will blight their lives for ever. They are more likely to regard it as an 'everyday problem'.[8] For many young people, the departure of a parent or the arrival of a stepparent and stepbrothers and sisters can be hugely positive. It is only when changes happen too fast, or when they all came at once, that they become hard for children to cope with.

This research concludes that a substantial majority of young people in the study had moved on from their parents' divorce after four years, and had become preoccupied with the challenges of their own lives. They did not want to be typecast as the children of divorced parents. The picture was not of sad children desperately wanting their parents to get back together but of people who accepted their reality as part of a divorced family. Until divorce is decentred, however, it will remain the chief point of categorization for young people, who appear to want to be understood in ways other than as victims of the damage done to them by divorce.

It is not inconsistent to argue both that lifelong marriage is the preferred family form for bringing up children and also that a child can thrive in a newly 'blended' family. Thatcher is clear that the evidence points to the need for children, wherever possible, to be brought up by their biolological parents[9] and, according to Beck-Gernsheim, each new 'multiparent patchwork' family grouping for a child of divorced parents will be built on the bones of a previous one: sadness is endemic within its creation.[10] However, this can overlook the energy that can come through a reconfiguration of relationships. Family life is not going to be improved solely by blaming divorce. Identifying wider social patterns of family behaviour provides a necessary backcloth for understanding the full significance of divorce within our society.

WHAT IS THE WIDER SOCIAL PICTURE?

Just like the children in the Neale, Flowerdew and Sanders study, I don't want to be defined by my divorce. I am a survivor rather than a victim of what has happened to me. Divorce is life-changing rather than life-threatening. It is a fallacy to assume that divorce can be properly understood only in terms of the damage that it does to people.

A survey, which questioned 3,515 adults (but did not scrutinise the impact on children), found that of those in the first two years since a split, 53 per cent of women felt relieved (men 46 per cent), 46 per cent of women felt liberated (men 37 per cent) and 31 per cent of women were happy (men 22 per cent). Shockingly, the report claims that although it is distressing, a break-up can also be a 'positive life change', with women better able to cope with all its stages than men. While women are more likely to feel relieved, liberated and happy, men are more likely to feel sad, devastated, betrayed, confused and even suicidal. Among both sexes, 57 per cent of those who agreed to separate in the last two years say they are happier now, while among those who broke up two or more years ago, 74 per cent are happier.[11]

Promoting family living is a wider issue than defending marriage. If all our energy is put into dealing with the pressures and strains on the nuclear family structure of marriage, we can miss the new ways of contemporary family living that are emerging through a wider repatterning of family living. Divorce is part cause and part symptom of a wider social realignment. It is now not possible to speak of a river (marriage) so much as a series of rivers (marriage, cohabitation, divorce, singleness) along which people travel during their lives.[12]

For people who have lived together before being married, marriage has ceased to be the rite of passage that it was in previous generations. It is often the birth of a child rather than getting married that makes the difference to people's patterns of lifestyle.

There has been an increase in the number and proportion of children born outside of marriage. In 1971 these children constituted 8 per cent of births, increasing to 22 per cent in 1981 and 34 per cent in 1995.[13] Cohabitation and civil law partnerships have created a relationship hierarchy that undercuts traditional church views on marriage. The marriage service is not a one-size-fits-all ritual of relationships. The creation of new family ties, in the form of a husband or wife, is no longer a matter of course but a freely chosen act, based on feelings and personal harmony. Marriage, then, needs to prove itself as the best option against a horizon of different possibilities.

THE DEBATE ABOUT THE SHAPE OF THE FAMILY IS UP FOR GRABS

The debate about the family, both in society and in the church, is cast in extreme and reactionary terms. Stories about the family seem to be negative (about family violence and failure to care properly for young and old), reformative (about renewal of family values) or nostalgic (asking where the 'good old days' have gone). Family, whatever that signifies, is presented as sacrosanct. The relationships between family members are seen as a microcosm of society and a prototype for all other social relations. The family unit is seen as the fundamental building block for society and a shock absorber of social change.

The role of the parent in today's family is seen as being non-negotiable. Parenting is replacing partnership as the backbone of modern family living.[14] The parental relationship within the family is idealized and even sentimentalized; it has been characterized as the last truly romantic relationship. This is illustrated by contemporary soap operas in which the claims of husband and wife are seen as temporal but the claims of parents are seen as absolute. Intergenerational relationships may collapse (my divorce is proof of that) but cross-generational relationships are absolute. A blood relationship between parent and child takes precedence over an intergenerational relationship between husband and wife.

As is often the case in a discussion where extreme positions are held, the reality is more fluid and open than might first seem apparent: the louder the defence, the more uncertain is the ground. There is no clear consensus, either in social or theological terms, as to what form the family might take. There is agreement on the role that family plays within society but not on the actual shape and structure of that family. My contention is that the central role of the family within society does not automatically presuppose a nuclear family structure. The nuclear family unit reached its zenith during the Industrial Revolution, when the family needed to form an economic unit with one partner (traditionally the male) earning a wage and one partner (traditionally the female) managing the home and family. A feminist perspective highlights the ongoing role of the woman in carrying this particular structure of family living by subjugating her role to the wage-earning male. The fewer women are prepared to do this, the more strain it will put on the structure of a nuclear family. This is now reflected in the divorce statistics, in that it is more often women who are initiating divorce proceedings. Three-fifths of the petitions for divorce come from the wives; more than two and a half times as many divorces were granted to women as to men in the early 1990s.[15]

As I have suggested, divorce is part symptom and part cause of a wider set of social issues, and once divorce is made the scapegoat, then attention can be deflected from underlying causes of marital breakdown. For example, electronic living creates a pressure on marriages that never previously existed. A survey of 1500 adults by Market Research Company TNS was commissioned by Sandra Davis, partner and head of family practice at the law firm Mischcon de Reya (the firm that acted for Diana, Princess of Wales in her divorce with Prince Charles). It found that electronic communications had made it easier to begin affairs and to keep them going. Internet sites such as www.friendsreunited.co.uk have allowed bored and disaffected spouses to revive old romances by email, away from the prying eyes of their partners.

Text messaging has made it easier than ever to arrange clandestine meetings, while the proliferation of sex chat rooms has created a whole new challenge to marital harmony: virtual infidelity. 46 per cent of those surveyed said they believed that e-mails, texting and chat rooms had led to a big rise in infidelity. Nearly 30 per cent admitted using electronic communications to flirt with potential partners or nurture an affair; of those, 22 per cent confessed to doing so every day, while 62 per cent did so once a week.[16]

There are particular and distinctive pressures on families in which both partners are out at work. Commercialization of child care can provide some of the answer, but children left both in a breakfast club and an after-school club can have as long a 'working day' as their parents. Given that the nuclear family, in its origins, is an economic unit, as soon as both partners begin to work, the economic rationale for the union begins to break down. This becomes particularly evident when (as was the case with Sarah and me) there are no children involved. In social and economic terms, the fact that we were married made little difference to how we lived our lives. We shared our home but, apart from this context of mutual support and accountability, we pursued twin-track careers and made different but overlapping lives for ourselves. The shape of the marriage reflected and legitimized the lifestyle choices we would have made anyway, had we remained single.

Our relationship was culturally shaped as well as individually chosen. In social terms, a family cannot be defined any more clearly than as a group of individuals related to one another by law or birth.

The term 'family' is very difficult to describe precisely. While everyone intuitively has a sense of what it means, the great diversity of family types makes it almost impossible to identify the family solely in terms of form. This left Sarah and me without guidance on how to shape our marriage and free to make the mistakes that led eventually to our divorce. We followed the ritual of marriage and forgot the reasons. In essence, ours was a marriage but not a family.

Discussion about the shape of a family falls into one of the two different camps. The more liberal perspective is relatively unconcerned about the form of a family, accepting uncritically almost any kind of caring adult relationship with or without children. Two-parent families, single-parent families, cohabiting adults and homosexual unions can be equally valid according to this view and ought to be legitimized in law, public policy and church life. From this perspective, family is defined almost exclusively in terms of function rather than in terms of shape and form. Proponents of this view can often minimize the negative consequences of family break-up. Divorce can be seen as a part of a quest for individual happiness and fulfilment, thus underemphasizing its effects on spouses and children.

The contrasting and more traditional perspective would accept only one form of family—the two-parent nuclear family system. This perspective can inadvertently advocate restrictive codes of behaviour, with limited empathy for those involved in family breakdowns, sometimes looking more to cast blame than to meet the needs of those affected by the breakdown. The proponents of the single family system can end up advocating a social code rather than a theological ideal. This perspective runs the risk of not appreciating the gifts and expanding role of women, idealizing the stay-at-home wife and mother. It does not recognize either the economic circumstances that often force women to work or the capabilities of women for work outside the home. In its rigid separation of parental roles, it can also minimize the role that fathers should play in caring for children. Much of this vision of the traditional family represents a middle-class, 18th-century, Western social structure rather than a biblical vision of the family. Beck-Gernsheim poses the question:

Should we stick to and consider as correct, normal and appropriate the traditional image of family as lifelong father, mother, and child unit? Should we regard other forms as incomplete and deviant, deficient and dysfunctional? Or on the contrary should the claims to precedence of the traditional form be rejected? Should more attention be paid to all the lifestyles and types of relationship that are developing outside what has traditionally been counted as traditional family? [17]

A BIBLICAL UNDERSTANDING OF FAMILY

The contemporary idea of the family as an isolated unit is a long way from the model of the extended family represented in the pages of scripture. The Bible is unequivocal about the importance of marriage but, other than the centrality of a monogamous and faithful relationship and the bringing up of children, is largely unprescriptive about what shape the family will take. The Christian perspective has more to say about the theological purpose than the socially constructed shape of the family unit. The four basic parameters for the family outlined in scripture are procreation and nurture, fidelity, monogamy and permanence.

Procreation and nurture: The heart of the marital relationship is a child, along with mutual edification and support. While the birth of children is not necessary to a definition of the family, it is within the safe confines of the marital bond between husband and wife that children are to be conceived, born and nurtured. God said to the man and woman, 'Be fruitful and multiply' (Genesis 1:28, NRSV). Another important aspect of Christian family life, mirrored in the church, is the function of education and nurture. After the summary of the law given in Deuteronomy 6:4–5, we are instructed to teach the commandments to our children: 'Recite them to your children and talk about them when you are at home and when you are away, when you lie down and when you rise' (v. 7, NRSV). The healthy family is also committed to helping each member discover and develop individual spiritual gifts. It is not threatened but rejoices with individual achievements and success.

Fidelity: Fidelity is the divine will for marriage. Jesus, quoting Genesis 2:24 ('Therefore a man leaves his father and his mother and clings to his wife, and they become one flesh', NRSV), concluded, 'Therefore what God has joined together, let no one separate' (Matthew 19:6, NRSV). The warning of the seventh commandment, prohibiting adultery (Exodus 20:14), underscores the exclusiveness of marriage, which God intends. Mutual devotion between husband and wife is a reflection of God's devotion to his people (Ephesians 5:21–33).

Monogamy: The consistent witness of the church is that marriage involves one man and one woman (Matthew 19:3–9; 1 Timothy 3:1–13). One measurement of the declining role of marriage is the National Survey of Sexual Attitudes and Lifestyles published in 1994. This found that, since the 1940s, the median age at which virginity was lost had dropped for females from 21 to 17 and for males from 20 to 17. Orthodox evangelical Christian teaching is that marriage is the appropriate context for full sexual intercourse, as it allows practical and emotional commitment to keep pace with physical expression of love.

Permanence: Marriage is meant to last a lifetime: people getting married are asked to be faithful to each other 'as long as [they] both shall live'. The permanence of marriage can be interrupted only by death or, in some rare instances, by divorce—for example, where unchastity is proven (Matthew 5:32). In this verse, Jesus tightened his contemporaries' thinking about divorce, because this offered protection to women who would otherwise have been economically vulnerable, away from their husband. The issue of a woman's economic dependence on her partner is still pertinent in understanding the fallout from divorce.

The Bible both acknowledges the reality and sanctions the

possibility of divorce. Jesus' veto on divorce was in the context of a debate about the teaching of Rabbis Shammai and Hillel, who argued over how the expression 'something indecent', found in Deuteronomy 24:1, should be interpreted. Rabbi Shammai saw divorce as always wrong. He made a strict interpretation of Deuteronomy 24:1, arguing that the sole ground for divorce was a grave matrimonial offence, 'something indecent'. Rabbi Hillel saw divorce as only sometimes wrong. He held a very permissive view (which was the common attitude of the day) and made a loose interpretation of the phrase in Deuteronomy 24:1 to mean 'any cause whatsoever'. Thus, 'something indecent' was interpreted in the widest possible sense, even to include trivial faults like burning the bread. Among the Hillelites, Rabbi Akiba went so far as to say that a man could divorce his wife if he found another woman who was more beautiful. Jesus cut across both of these positions. His prohibition of divorce (see also Luke 16:18) was to protect women who would otherwise be left unnecessarily vulnerable to a husband who wanted to end the marriage for any reason of his own.

The Bible is also clear about the value of singleness, for not everyone marries. Thatcher suggests that discouragement of marriage in the Bible is probably stronger than its encouragement.[18] This neither depreciates the value of marriage nor negates the general truth of Genesis 2:18: 'It is not good that the man should be alone' (NRSV). Jesus lived a single life, as did Paul and many of the disciples. Singleness does not mean, however, a life of isolation: single people are not to live their lives in a social vacuum. Human beings were created to live in community, not in isolation. Thus, the church has an important obligation and responsibility to all people, both married and single, to act as an extended family and to welcome strangers.

MARRIAGE PREPARATION

Marriage preparation in the church can be decontextualized from these wider social influences when it concentrates solely on the relationship skills of the people getting married (for example, listening attentively, saying sorry and not putting the other person down). Couples are told that when they are married they need to work hard to maintain the romance that brought them together. This ignores the wider social context that puts the marriage under extra strain in the first place: it is akin to smartening the rowing boat while ignoring the change in the weather.

Exploring the wider context would include questions such as:

- What is the role of grandparents in day-to-day child care?
- Do husband and wife have equal claims on a working career?
- What claim does a previous marriage have on one of the partners if it was ended through no fault of their own?
- What is the loyalty of a new wife to children of a previous marriage?
- What if you have a child but no spouse?
- If one partner gets a job promotion in another town, should the family move or should s/he try commuting and a 'weekend marriage' (with children kept in the same school)?

Church teaching on marriage can be strong on God's intention and purpose but offer less help with everyday life and living. There is a story that gives an analogy for the decontextualized marriage preparation of the type I am describing. Two people are having a picnic when they see a body floating down the nearby river. They jump in and save the person's life. Five minutes later, the same thing happens and again they save the person's life. When they see a third body, instead of jumping into the river one of them starts to run upstream. 'Where are you going?' his friend cries. 'To find the person who is throwing the bodies into the river!' is the reply.

Marriage preparation that focuses entirely on the rekindling of romantic love is like jumping into the river to rescue the floating bodies. It ignores the wider social context that leads to the situation in the first place.

The blankness of marriage preparation based on the single idea 'Don't get divorced' is the mirror image of Christian teaching on sexual ethics often given to young people: 'When you are tempted, don't.' This type of approach to young people's sex education gives no consideration to the wider issue of a developing sense of identity through a growth in sexual awareness. Zygmunt Bauman uses the term 'liquid society' to describe the fact that we live, work and (maybe) socialize in different areas.[19] Liquid society means that more constructs of behaviour than in previous generations are individually chosen rather than socially predetermined. Young people have to make sense of the commercialization of sexual identity in the same way that married couples need to shape a sense of permanence and stability within a liquid society.

The assumption of romantic love is, in itself, a culturally defined social construct. There is a lot to be learnt from other cultures about good practice in marriage. I lived in India for two years as a part of a programme with the Church Mission Society, and learnt to respect the social practice of marriages arranged within families. Arranged marriages have been caricatured by the Western media as a situation in which poor young women are forced into a relationship against their will. However, arranged marriages can happen with the full consent and involvement of the two parties involved. The ethos of an arranged match is that you love the person you marry; the ethos of a love marriage is that you marry the person you love, and there is no evidence that a love marriage is automatically happier than a mutually agreed arranged marriage. Part of the work I did while in India was to teach in a boarding school for girls. I met intelligent teenage women there for whom arranged marriages were as much the norm as love marriages were for me. Their disregard for love marriages paralleled the Western media's suspicion of arranged marriages. The girls teased me, wanting to know why I would not consult my parents over whom I should marry. As far as they were concerned, their parents were the people who knew and loved them best and it did not make sense for me to exclude them from the most important decision of their lives.

TENSIONS IN FAMILY LIVING

If it is true that there are different patterns of family life and if, at the same time, the nuclear structure is taken as the baseline norm, then stresses are inevitable. Women who stay at home, women who go out to work and fathers (following a divorce) occupy the central parenting role of the family differently. Each is squeezed by a tight adherence to a model of nuclear family. Some families will move back towards an extended family unit, drawing on the help of grandparents or buying in, in the shape of a nanny or au pair, the extra people needed to support the parents' dual incomes. Other families will struggle. More often than not, mothers continue to take responsibility for raising the children.

There are issues for mothers who stay at home with child care responsibilities: they can end up bored and frustrated.[20] There are different concerns for mothers who go out to work. Between the late 1970s and the mid 1990s, the proportion of married women, with children younger than five years old, who were involved in paid work doubled from 27 per cent to 54 per cent.[21] Working women had the economic freedom to consider life beyond marriage. A research project from Vrije University in Amsterdam drew findings from a database of more than 2000 people, including 1000 divorced women. The study concluded that the probability of divorce was in direct correlation to the number of hours a woman worked. Women working full-time were 29 per cent more likely to get divorced than those who stayed at home and raised children.[22]

Fathers are left vulnerable by the power dynamics if the marriage ends in divorce. Bob Geldof suggests that family law, as it currently stands, does not work. It is rarely of benefit to the child and promotes injustice, conflict and unhappiness on a massive scale. He talks about the emergence of non-traditional family structures:

If the later 20th century saw the transformation of women's lives, then the 21st century is seeing the transformation of men's lives, and by definition the lives of their children. Nearly half the workforce is female and men now hold a different view of parenting... [there is]... confused thinking, lying at the heart of family law, that allows it to be unjustly weighted in favour of women... There are no studies which suggest that a child brought up by a man (as I was) displays any psychological or emotional characteristics different to one raised by a woman. [23]

TRANSFORMATION

Hayman writes that it isn't divorce or living in a stepfamily that damages children or hurts adults; it is badly managed divorce that does the harm. [24] Horror stories about stepfamilies cloud the fact that it is often the process of transition rather than the newly reshaped family that does most harm to the child. Divorce turns children into 'little adults' who anxiously protect their fragile parents, instead of being protected as they are in 'intact' families. Divorce forces children to guard parental secrets—protecting Mum by not telling Dad, or vice versa. Children are damaged when one parent consistently talks the other partner down, or when the child is used as an emotional go-between for the two parents. Based on a national study of the children of divorce, surveying 1500 young adults from both divorced and intact families and interviewing more than 70 of them at length, Marquardt concluded that there is no such thing as a 'good divorce' when children are forced into an arbitrating role between the two parents. [25]

Hayman writes that the risks that children face in relation to divorce are often less to do with actual parental separation and more to do with the behaviour of the parents. The key factor is the conflict that can occur before, during and after separation, and the impact that badly managed conflict has on parents and parent–child relationships.[26] Katzenberg writes that it can take up to five years for parents to be able to talk politely to each other about the children without being unduly affected; he talks of the need to stay civil throughout, otherwise parents' evenings, birthdays, sports days and so on become unbearable.[27]

It is possible for a particular family to fit the traditional family model of husband and wife with biological children, yet totally miss the mark of spiritual and social enrichment that is called for in scripture. A traditional family form is no guarantee against neglect or abuse. Mutual love can be absent in nuclear families as much as it can be present in non-nuclear families. Many of the Bible's great teachings on the Christian home are offered in the context of non-traditional settings, even dysfunctional homes, like those of Abram, Jacob and David. In contemporary terms, the conduct of some of the biblical protagonists could be considered outrageous. Abram pimped his wife Sarah in the hope of safe passage out of Egypt (Genesis 12:13). Jacob was married to two sisters, Rachel and Leah, at the same time (29:14–30) and David committed adultery with Bathsheba (2 Samuel 11:4). Jesus encouraged his disciples to abandon their families to follow him (Luke 14:26). Biblically-based family values are not for the exclusive benefit of one particular type of family configuration.

Statistics that scapegoat one-parent families ignore the fact that the disadvantages are often economic rather than family-based. Lawler says that it is 'the feminisation and childrenisation of poverty that causes a lot of any of the disadvantages to a child being brought up by a single parent'.[28] Simpson suggests that doom-mongering and negativity about single-parent families is an example of societal misogyny, given that women head 91 per cent of the single-parent families in the UK.[29] The number of one-person households has grown by 31 per cent in the past 30 years, while the population has increased by only 5 per cent. In 2002, a third of all households were single-parented.[30]

Thatcher talks of churches worldwide having much to do in recognizing stepfamilies as a growing family form. He talks of the need for the church to support 'blended families', which might include a whole new configuration of relationships—for example, an able-bodied person caring for a declining friend or partner, or single-parent families where the parent is trying to be both mother and father to their children.[31] Single-parent families can draw others into the parenting process. My friend Annie (who writes in the next chapter) has 'imported' me on occasions as a male role model. Cox and Desforges write that it is possible to create a new family— a fluid, extended family that echoes but is quite different from the old, static, extended family.[32] Children can have wider networks, perhaps a range of different siblings—not just full siblings, but half-siblings and stepsiblings—and a range of grandparents, step-grandparents and aunties and uncles. Children can even gain from having four loving parents around them. This fluid, extended family then becomes the UK cultural version of the African proverb that it 'takes a whole village to raise a child'.

In Nick Hornby's novel *About a Boy*, twelve-year-old Marcus feels relieved to have become a part of a newly formed, non-biological, blended family. He and his (single-parent) mum are now tapped into a wider social network than they had been previously:

'I was really scared because I didn't think two was enough, and now there aren't two any more. There are loads. And you're better off that way… It's like those acrobatic displays… when you stand on top of loads of people in a pyramid. It doesn't really matter who they are, does it, as long as they're there and you don't let them go away without finding someone else.'

The novel's narrator also comments, 'In London… people came at each other from all sorts of odd angles. You could create little patterns of people that wouldn't have been possible if his mum and dad hadn't split up.'[33]

In India, I learnt that a child might live with the best-positioned member of the family both in terms of location (in particular, access to schools) and money. This practice assumes the idea of extended family as the norm. The blanket assumption that children are best raised within separate nuclear economic units ignores the fact that the decline of the viability of the nuclear family unit need not mean a weakening of the central and pivotal role of the family within society. The values of family living are too important to be contained by the institution of marriage alone.

TO CONCLUDE

If people see their own situations reflected back at them through the scapegoat, they will either criticize too harshly or accept too readily what has happened. I have been told from a pulpit that 'some, like our own [culture], have such low, casual, take-it-or-leave-it attitudes toward marriage as to make the biblical vision seem ludicrous to most people'. It was a silly comment, unfair to those who have struggled unsuccessfully to keep a marriage together, but it highlights how easy it is to caricature the debate. I can respond defensively when asked for money by someone who is homeless because I see my own vulnerabilities reflected back at me. The wider community can respond defensively when confronted by divorce for similar reasons. Dinner invitations dry up because of the host's desire not to have an odd number at the table. Friends are caught between conflicting stories. Congregations are embarrassed and divorcé(e)s ashamed.

It is a part of the self-preservation and propagation of any society to define appropriate behaviour by what does not fit into its own constructs: there are so many boxes, spaces and paths that are predefined. Foucault talks of society's need to describe certain behaviour as 'madness'.[34] My divorce and Foucault's 'madness' both expose notions of conventionality and break social patterns of conformity. Divorce is akin to 'a work of art [that] opens a void, a moment of silence, a question without answer, provokes a breach without reconciliation where the world is forced to question itself and in the time of that work, swamped in madness, the world is made aware of its guilt'.[35]

My situation does not fit into underlying assumptions of happiness and well-being. In order to preserve notions of continuity and stability, social norms and expectations distance themselves from what cannot be forced back into line or categorized by a standard form or order. Idealized forms of family then feed on divorce as proof and justification of their own position within society.

Foucault writes, 'The pressure of conformity shapes how an experience is understood and forms a constitutive moment of definition. It draws the exterior edge, the line of dissolution, the contour against the void.'[36] If this comment could be translated into the context of the church, it would be saying that the institution needs to distance itself in order to define itself. This is correct if we think solely in terms of the law and of the church as an unredeemed organization. What I need from the church is a grace-filled welcome alongside a law-shaped definition. I need this to reconnect with the person I am, to be helped through the fallout from the divorce and to allow the next stage of my life to be defined by God's love rather than my hurt feelings.

DOS AND DON'TS

I need to thank a lot of people who are helping me through this twilight period. I will do so in this chapter, which is in the form of a pastoral à la carte menu card. It is a simplified list of dos and don'ts, illustrating how you might respond to a friend or family member facing the prospect of a divorce. Each section ends with some practical reflections. It is one thing for someone to learn from their own mistakes; I am inviting you to do the clever thing and learn from mistakes made by someone else. I include comments in each section from Annie, who has been through the experience herself and been a good friend to me in the process. She writes of her own situation, 'Even though he left me, I have a responsibility for what happened and I don't want to blame my ex because that does not help anyone. I want to learn from it all to see how I can make things better for the future.'

It is easy to generalize and hypothesize about divorce as something that happens to other people, but imagine yourself face-to-face with someone like Annie or myself and think how you might respond. Friends and family are always drawn into the process and have to make their own decisions about how to behave. In one sense, it is an emotional minefield: single words or expressions uttered by friends have plunged me into a deep gloom. I mind when people talk about divorce because I feel stigmatized. I mind when people do not talk about it because I feel ignored. In another sense, though, it will be easy for you to help someone like me because you can hardly make the situation any worse than it already is.

Getting alongside and helping someone to face up to the prospect of divorce is slow and patient work, but there are aspects to any divorce that allow for some general principles to be drawn. It is difficult to stay impartial and remain equal friends to both parties;

however, this should not mean that you underestimate the help you can give. Don't give up too quickly on the marriage, but allow the person to decide for themselves how to deal with the situation. Finally, don't talk the person's partner down. They will either not want you to do so or they will be doing it perfectly well for themselves.

DIFFERENT PATTERNS BUT COMMON THREADS

My story is only one among any number of different scenarios. Some people have come out of a marriage that they saw as essentially good, and grieve deeply the loss of the relationship; for others, separation has brought release from a troubled and painful situation. Some have spent months or even years fighting to save their marriage; others have moved swiftly through the process, wanting only to get it over with as soon as possible. There are endless variations on this theme. It takes a minimum of three years to recover from a broken heart, but it can also take as long to heal as it did to break: destructive habits built up over a number of years can take the same amount of time to unravel. I have only just started this journey; I will need to be patient with myself and trust in God. Time is one of the healing properties of the Holy Spirit.

A divorced person may be someone who drifts slowly loose from what they consider to be a lifeless marriage. A divorced person may be the one who leaves the marriage, perhaps quite literally walking out. People who leave a marriage deal with guilt and responsibility in equal measures, while people who are left deal with the sense of rejection and betrayal. Sometimes separation and divorce are a relief and release from a painful and difficult situation. Living with a partner who is physically or psychologically abusive—or even with someone who simply seems unwilling to make any of the running in the relationship—is debilitating.

Those with a Christian faith will stick with a difficult marriage far longer than those with no faith because they believe that the relationship is God's will. When they finally cut loose, there can be a sense of relief. Mixed in with pleasure at newfound freedom, though, there may be guilt and misgivings about whether it was right to leave, and questions about whether all that could have been done to save the marriage had been done. There is still grief but it is for the marriage that now will never be, for the family that is broken, for children who won't be born. Experience of divorce depends not only on reasons and circumstances but also on personality, beliefs and values, the internal and external resources available, and so on. The experience also changes over time: 20 years on, the view will inevitably be quite different from the one in the immediate aftermath.

Despite these many differences, it is clear from conversations with people in a wide variety of situations that there are common threads running though the many different weaves. Whatever the particulars of the circumstances, at the heart of the matter is the tragedy of a broken relationship, and this is not just any relationship but the one we took to be the relationship of our life. For better or worse, this is the person we chose to be our life's companion. Into this relationship we invested our hopes, our dreams and our very selves. When such a relationship breaks down, the world closes in and we are left alone with a volatile mixture of emotions.

Messy emotions don't fit into neat packages. Both within the church and in the wider society, there is no one-size-fits-all divorce. Everyone has his or her own version of grief, which, like DNA, is specific and particular to each person's life. A decision to divorce is never based on politeness and good manners. There are endless examples of great cruelty and blind stupidity in equal measures. There are women lured by the prospect of something better, and feckless men who have children by two different women and are now wondering about a third. One woman was told by her husband that he was going to leave her on the same day that she told him she was pregnant. She said to me, 'Life is too long to argue—I don't want to have a whole 24 hours when I am angry with someone.' It is a good sentiment, but she is still angry.

Some people have been in marriages that crumbled before the wedding photos came back from the photographer. One person I talked with told me how she was stood up on her wedding day: she had a divorce without even having had the marriage. She told me that she thought it would take ten years to get over (and it did). Another person said that he had made a mistake on the honeymoon and filed for divorce when they returned home. Another friend saw a relationship trail away after three years of living together. There was no one reason, but his partner appeared to have lost interest. They were never married but a broken heart is always a broken heart and there are never any winners in the process.

As I've already said, I call those of us who have been divorced the 'society of the dispossessed'. Members of this society have an emotional pragmatism coming out of a shared set of experiences that do not need any explanation to other members. It is plain that some of those who best understand what I mean when I am talking about divorce are people who have experienced divorce or something comparable. There is a homing instinct that draws me towards others in my position. When I talk with other divorced people, I am able to recognize that within all these different stories there are still enough similarities and comparisons to be able to put down some general markers of behaviour.

To consider
1. How do you avoid being too definitive and prescriptive about what you think the divorced person should do?
2. How can you be clear in what you think while still making the other person feel accepted by you?
3. How do you support someone without making them feel condemned as an individual?

4. Can you ask direct questions that give responsibility to the divorced person? How do they feel about the situation? Is there anything they would like you to do to help?
5. How can you mix sympathy with practicality? Overconcern can make the situation worse. It can make the other person feel that things must be really bad for you to behave as you are doing.

IT IS NOT EASY TO BE FRIENDS TO BOTH PARTIES

I have cut contact with Sarah: this has been possible only because we have not had children together. The die is cast and I do not see myself being able to translate our relationship as lovers to a newly structured friendship, meeting for lunch from time to time and asking each other how things are going. She is my wife and lover, or nothing. This decision may not match up to the ideal forgiving self I might want to be, but I do not have anything more within me to give to the situation. We do not have a dog to argue over or a CD collection to be divided. We have a flat that needs to be sold, but my brother Edward tells me that he will manage the sale for me. He says, 'Selling a flat is selling a flat and ending a marriage is ending a marriage. You need to sell a flat, so give me the power of attorney.' I do just that. He later tells me to go off and join a gym. 'You've been saving for a rainy day,' he says. 'Face it, this is your rainy day!' He has got a point.

I have also distanced myself from mutual friends. There are two reasons for doing this. The first is that I am being crabby and unreasonable and taking it out on those closest to me. I snapped a friendship in one sentence by asking the person to choose between the two of us: it put her in an impossible position. She felt angry with me for giving her such an ultimatum and felt that I was judging her for wanting to support Sarah. One couple who have spent time with us both also think that I am unreasonable in wanting them to take sides. They see themselves as wanting to help; I see them as wanting to help on their own terms. They think they are being reasonable; I feel that they are distancing themselves. I am terrified that they are legitimizing the situation by wanting to be friends to us both, and I am not yet ready for that. I tell them that the issue is not about them and their sense of friendship; it is about Sarah and me, and neutrality is still a judgment.

Annie wrote this of her situation:

One of the hardest times for me, and a memory that keeps returning, was when a supposed friend stopped being my friend. Without explanation, she just started avoiding me. It was a time when I needed friends more than anything; I had already lost so much. I suppose that it was difficult for her to be friends with both sides as she had known my ex for longer. It would have taken great strength for her to support me too.

My reticence with friends is because I need to start the process of putting some distance between myself and what has happened, and to build up new moments in time unaffected by what now needs to become my past. I need the insulation of people who do not know my history. I want conversations that have no route back to Sarah. I want to create new spaces that I can count as my own.

Adrian runs the café where I sit quietly in the corner, reading and writing. I spend a weekend helping him to build a brick wall in his garden. On another occasion, I get up early to help him make sandwiches. It does not matter what we are doing together: the point is that they are new moments in time. He has become friend enough to want to invite me over to his house. These types of occasion give me glimpses of what it might be like living in the present moment, free from a brutalized past.

Eve came to Cambridge with Addie her daughter and Oscar my godson. The three of us went punting even though it was raining. It was a funny, crazy, unnecessary thing to do and we all got soaked.

The weather was miserable but it seemed incumbent upon us to make the most of the situation. The past has gone and the future is unclear, and so we make the most of the present. Andy moves into my new house as a lodger. We sit and drink whisky late into the night and have male-type conversations about the prospects for the season for his football club (Huddersfield Town). He never met Sarah. This is important to me. I am grateful for conversations that ask nothing of me and allow me to create new emotional spaces.

The upheaval from a divorce is simultaneously emotional and material: external things become symbols of internal feelings. My grandmother gave me a television long before I had even met Sarah. It comforts me even when I am not watching a programme. It represents the fact that I had a life before my marriage. I dislike the large mirror across the living-room wall because it was a wedding present. A newly ironed shirt represents my determination to make the best of the day ahead. Books and photographs go into a box—temporary and in transit before the future takes shape. I invite to supper two people who knew us both, and I buy an entirely new set of cutlery. There is a future out there somewhere, and a John Lewis set of knives represents this hope.

I can see a similar pattern of behaviour in a woman whose husband has died. I want to replace memories with new experiences; she wants to replace memories by reshaping the geography of the house. She goes through the house, slowly replacing pieces of furniture. The house she shared with her husband shapes her memories. She wants new furniture with no history of her marriage attached to it. Her children are confused and feel distanced by what she is doing. They expect her to adopt the more passive mourning ritual associated with a grieving widow.

I do not want to spread the pain. I do not want my negative thoughts to affect and infect other people, so I try to hermetically seal the whole process. For a period, I do not even want to talk about what is going on because it gives a sterner reality to the whole thing. As soon as a thought is articulated, it takes on a life of its own. This is denial—the first of Kübler-Ross's five stages of grief, denial, anger, bargaining, depression and acceptance.[1]

The idea that there are different stages of grief helps me to understand what I am going through. These stages are not stops on some prescribed linear timeline in grief. On some days I seem to be feeling some of each and every one of the emotions listed. Eventually I will progress more fully through anger, bargaining, depression and acceptance. In the meantime, I can recognize different people at different stages in the process of recovery. One friend describes her 'denial' stage as the sense of being caught in chaos (internal) and her 'anger' stage as feeling like walking through ruins (external). At the 'denial' stage, she was numb and found it hard to talk to people about what had happened. Now, at the 'anger' stage, she does not want to stop talking. She needs to talk in order to put the breakdown of her marriage into context: in effect, her talking is helping to create a new reality against which she can interpret her marriage breakdown. I am not yet ready for that. At this point, I am still too scared of regularizing the situation.

For the time being, 'denial' is my way of coping. I am still suspended by the glazed assumption that divorce happens only to other people. I don't mind; shock is God's anaesthetic. It allows me to adjust to what is happening and to build up a store of reserves for what lies ahead. I am not going to allow myself to be hurried through this first stage because I sense that I am going to feel a lot worse once the full process of grief sets in. This is the best emotional state that I will be in for a while. One of the cruellest things about suffering is its power to isolate the sufferer: in the words of H. Williams, 'People are happy together but miserable alone.'[2]

Set against this emotional blockade that I am erecting, other people have to find their own natural level. Some friends are strong enough to ignore my defensiveness and are able to offer their own comfort. Marianne is a long-standing friend who lives in deepest rural Suffolk. She and I have written to each other over a number of years. She invites herself for a coffee and reads out some of the letters I wrote to her while I was still married. The point she is making is that the marriage I had with Sarah is not as good or as bad as I might now think. Writing teaches me about myself. It prevents me from sleepwalking through the process. It is an instinct as much as it is a choice. I wrote my way through my marriage partly by completing my doctorate and partly by writing endless letters to family and friends; now I am writing my way through my divorce.

Sarah and I both need support as much as the other. We both need people who have the patience, energy and sympathy to re-negotiate both sets of relationships. The situation is a volatile mixture of personalities, pragmatism and principles. My confidence has been knocked and, as a result, I read a script into people's behaviour that they do not intend to be there. Some of those who were friends to us both during the marriage have been drawn more to her than to me (or the other way round). My untidy self growls at this, but my ideal self recognizes that it is not a value judgment on me but an evolution of friendship that will follow its own natural course. Others draw back from both of us because the situation is asking more of them than they are willing to give: they don't want to take sides. My crabby self sees this as double betrayal, but I can recognize that they are simply being true to their own reality within the situation. Everything has changed with this divorce; things need to find their own natural level and not be harassed or chased into one extreme position or another. Justin goes round to Sarah and helps her put up shelves in her new flat. That is natural to the relationship that he has with her. I wish he hadn't told me that this is what he did, but I am still glad about what he has done.

To consider
1. How might you show your concern and support to the one, without talking the other person down?
2. What support can you offer if you do not agree with what the person has done?

3. How can you offer friendship to both parties in the divorce?
4. Can you help the other person work out what to do (I am still not sure!) without doing their thinking for them?
5. How do you encourage patience—without saying that time is a great healer! This is like saying to someone with flu that they will get better. It does not help in the immediate here and now.

DON'T ASSUME THERE IS NOTHING YOU CAN DO

Friends take different roles. Andy, my lodger, has the priceless gift of focusing on the present moment. He texts me to say that he has lost the key to the house and to ask me where I am and whether I can let him back in. I am relieved when I get his text. It means that I am still a part of a network of different relationships. Casual social text messaging is intimacy without engagement and suits me at the moment. At this stage, I am relieved to have a form of communication that does not require any level of emotional literacy.

A friend, Simon, rings periodically to find out how I am. He tells me that every time he asks me that question, I reply with a comment about Sarah. I tell him, that is my way of making sense of what has happened. Simon says I need to unpick my feelings from hers. The breakdown of the marriage has left me second-guessing what she might be feeling. Ironically, my thoughts and feelings have become more entwined with her than ever before. Simon wants to disentangle the ravelled threads, so he comes back at me again and again with the same simple and single question: 'What is it that you want to do?' In time, I hope that I will be able to answer him.

My family react to the situation like a pack of wolves that sees one of their own being hurt: they close round, wanting to defend me. They are stunning. My marriage dissolves and they change shape to absorb the impact. Edward, my brother, asked me what he could do to help. I explained that I had no notion of the etiquette of divorce. I did not know how to react to what was happening. I asked if we could meet to discuss different options that were open to me, and so we do just that. I sit round a table with my siblings, with a cup of coffee and bits of paper, and brainstorm about what might be the best thing for me to do next. It is virgin territory for all of us and so we talk together. These evenings do not require a high level of emotional intimacy but give me the support I need. I am out of my depth and the people who are helping me most are those who are clear and unsentimental about what they think. The practical tips that these sessions generate are illuminating and helpful but what is paramount is that I can draw on my wider family to step into the emotional gaps.

Catherine, my sister, cuts me a key to her house and offers to decorate the spare bedroom in a colour of my choice. I can come and go whenever I want. I don't use it but I am glad that the option is there. I also like the freedom she gives me to appear unexpectedly in her house on Saturday nights, when I might otherwise be sitting at home alone. Pip, a friend from university, says that friends are not scripted in as having a role. She feels that I am bottling up my feelings and she is worried because I am having long evenings at home on my own and won't confide in other people. What she wants me to know is that I am not the only one getting hurt in the process. Her identification with me, as someone also affected but outside the situation, is the most valuable thing that she has to offer.

A clear opinion helps me more than soft sympathy. In the immediate period following the death of my father, my mother talked about being helped by two complete strangers. The first was a widower. He introduced himself to her at a party with the words, 'Torture, isn't it!' Then he talked about something else. He understood enough to know that words were not going to alleviate the situation. The second person was a woman she met while walking her dog. This woman, herself also a widow, replied briskly to my mother's story, 'You have a dog! You have a Christian faith! You will be all right!' In a similar way, I was most helped by the people confident enough to step into the space that might embarrass others.

Friends Ed and Modchick visit me and see that I have a framed photo prominently on display. She asks me, 'Why?' Then she tells me bluntly to forget Sarah and starts talking about something else. Rick has a meal with Sarah. He tells me the same thing. He looks after me; he invites me away for weekends in Norfolk, but we rarely refer to Sarah after that first conversation.

Annie writes this of her situation:

Because I have children, I was most concerned that things continued along normally for them. I was worried that it would be more difficult for them to keep up with their friends. I had less time to run them around to after-school activities and invite their friends over after school, because I had to go back to work full time. It was so comforting when a friend's father invited my son to play football in the park, and so helpful when a friend offered one of my children a lift to a shared activity. I was so appreciative if my children were included. Also, I wanted my children to be around other two-parent families. I thought that this example would be good for them. It would have been easy for me simply to hang around with mainly other single friends.

It is sometimes difficult attending events previously attended as a couple—parties, weddings (obviously), school events and the like; a phone call before these types of occasions has been greatly appreciated.

To consider
1. How are you going to offer clear, simple and honest feedback (while avoiding 'I told you so')?
2. Are there any practical things that you can do to make things better (such as meals, invitations, or phone calls)? Offers of help that are little and often are better than occasional but extravagant gestures of assistance.

3. Would you invite someone to dinner without worrying that you have an odd number of people sitting round the table?
4. Is there anything you can give the other person? (A film on DVD or video will always be appreciated.)
5. Are you happy to listen, without telling the person to 'pull themselves together'?
6. Are you happy to do 'normal' things with people so that they don't feel they always have to talk about their divorce?
7. Can you offer a child a lift or a game of football now and again?

DON'T GIVE UP TOO QUICKLY ON THE MARRIAGE

A marriage is more durable than people might expect. There is no pride in the end of a marriage. I felt as if I would do anything, be anyone or put up with any number of indignities to return the situation to how it was before. It is important for me to do this if only, in time, to have the psychological justification to be able to walk away. The centrality of marriage in the Christian tradition means that I cling on to hope long after it has slipped like sand through my fingers. It is a period of quiet desperation. If everything is forgivable, then nothing is definitive. There are some fabulous examples of faithfulness in which people have negotiated long periods apart, even sometimes actually being divorced before returning to the marriage. The quiet dignity of one partner who keeps open the possibility of reconciliation, and the genuine repentance of another who wants a further opportunity to make their marriage work, are both testimonies to the redemptive power of a hard-fought love. The fact that marriage ended in divorce for both Annie and me does not mean that this should be so for others.

Annie wrote this of her situation:

Hurt and humiliated as I was, I still tried to work things out. I feel sure that I tried as hard as I could to make it work, and I am now comforted to know that I behaved correctly. It was a funny time: someone from church used to visit us to see if we were OK. My children were 1 and 3, and I could see that he was furious with my ex. It was still early days and I was grappling with the pain and shock. I wanted to forgive my ex because I knew it would release me, but the man said that I only need to forgive someone if they recognize what they have done and ask for forgiveness. This didn't really help me, as it was too early. It also seemed inadvertently blaming, which built up barriers against getting back together. People do separate and find ways to get back together and this should be encouraged. Keeping open and forgiving for as long as possible should be encouraged.

To consider

1. Can you be sure that every option to save the marriage has been tried? Has the other person considered counselling?
2. How can you let people go at their own pace without allowing them to wallow?
3. Are you able to meet and talk with the other person?
4. If there are children involved, would you be able to look after them so that the two parents could meet and talk together?
5. How can you combine sympathy with practicality? It can be a mistake to feed grief with too much oxygen. It will just carry on expanding.
6. Can you avoid taking sides, instead encouraging forgiveness and tolerance?

THE PERSON HAS TO DEAL WITH IT THEMSELVES

However difficult the situation was within my marriage, I feel worse now that it has ended and I am left sitting on my own, drawing virtual companionship from familiar characters in a TV soap opera. There was a stage when I would have gone anywhere and done or said anything to save the marriage. Now I find myself in a place beyond people's company and conversation. In the Bible, Job's friends were the most helpful before they started to tell him what to do and were happy simply to sit in silence with him. People are lining up ready to spend time with me or talk with me—weekends in the country or dinners in London are on offer—but none of that is what I need. I have gone into a period of hibernation. I realize that pretending I have a social life by sitting in people's front rooms in different parts of the country is no answer to what has happened to me. Nouwen writes that if I cannot fully face or replace the experience of loneliness with contented solitude, if I use people and activities to avoid the pain of being alone, then my personhood and individuality will remain distorted.[3] Relationships are influential to personhood but they cannot replace what I have lost. They can help to reshape but they will not define who I am.

I wrote the following entry in my journal:

I am spending long evenings on my own. I paint a smile on my face during the week and I get to Friday night knowing that I will not talk to anyone over the weekend. I am having an endless succession of grotty, lonely, damp weekends. I am simultaneously comforted and frightened by the silences. There is no social stigma attached to loneliness if people do not realize that that is what you are feeling. It does not matter to other people that I have been on my own over the weekend because no one will know on Monday what I have done since Friday. The less I tell them, the better, and the more fun they assume my weekend has been.

I need empty spaces—back in the house from work at 5pm, sitting in a pristine clean room on my own and not knowing what to do. I read an article in the newspaper and then it is 5.10. I put my sheets on to wash and then it is 5.20 and I am still on my own. On one occasion, I went out for a run, came back, showered, looked round the house and then went out for another run. I will have weekend after weekend of dull loneliness.

This is a painful, frightening and lonely period of time for me. I stand in supermarket queues wishing the process would take longer, because once it is finished I will need to think of something else to do. Some nights, I give up even trying to sleep, and watch films and videos late into the night. There is a surreal quality to being awake at 3am, watching an obscure game of football from Argentina that happens to be on the sports channel. I am living in my head and no one can tell me how to behave. This is my reality.

Annie wrote this of her situation:

I was determined to get through that period. I appreciated being invited out, but I also remember long evenings in by myself. I started smoking, not eating properly and daydreaming. At least when I eventually came out of this phase, I was a little thinner! It definitely took close to two years.

To consider
1. How can you support rather than protect the other person? (There is no getting round the solitude of divorce.)
2. Ask the person what help they would like: no one will know the answer better than them. It makes them the author of their own situation.
3. Don't try to hurry people through the healing process. It will be a long time before they want to be introduced to any prospective new partner.
4. How can you help someone trust to their own healing process? I feel a great sense of achievement at the end of each day—I have lived another whole 24 hours!

DON'T TALK THE OTHER PERSON'S PARTNER DOWN

People sometimes want to show their loyalty to me by criticizing Sarah. These types of conversations leave me feeling tight and tense inside. She is the same woman I chose to marry and it is important to me that circumstances should not alter the integrity of that decision. I have looked elsewhere in this book at the difference between marriage by covenant and marriage by contract. Within the ethos of covenant, there is no reason why I should think any less of Sarah because of what has happened between the two of us. When people are angry with her, it unnerves me because it feels as if they are slighting the decisions that I made back on my wedding day. It adds to the sinking feeling of helplessness—the feeling that things really are out of my control. I feel that if anyone is to be angry it is I, and if I am not angry then neither should they be; everyone has their own coping mechanisms and away from me they can be as angry as they want to be. However, I have enough to handle without having to deal with other people's feelings as well as my own. At times it feels as if I am responding to people responding to me. How do I deal with one person who is full of hurt, anger, kindness and opinions? She wants answers to questions that I am not yet ready to ask. Another person is practical, caring and forthright to the point of bluntness. He can leave me feeling battered by his relentless summation of my situation.

The question that I am asked most regularly is why it happened. People react to my divorce as they might do to an item of news reported on Radio 4. What happened? Why did it happen? Who is to blame? People want reasons and, if I do not give them any, they will make up their own. One person tells me that my marriage broke down because I was spending too much time doing 'acts of charity' for others. Another person tells me that I married the wrong woman. At this stage it seems to be all about people's opinions. In the absence of my own reasons, some of the explanations people offer are absurd. I shrug my shoulders, look philosophical and tell them that sometimes things happen just because they do. I am not yet ready to believe that things happen for a purpose.

It is perfectly natural for people to want to make sense of events. Divorce is a public story and other people need to process it for themselves. When Moses asked the name of God, God replied, 'I am who I am' (Exodus 3:14). God's name is mysterious because he is unknown, but Moses feels that this reply is not going to help him once he gets to Egypt. He continues to complain that the children of Israel are not going to believe that God is on their side (4:1). In my situation, people echo Moses' request in asking me for clear and certain explanations.

Annie writes this of her situation:

Friends talking down my ex was not very productive. It was easy for them to do and maybe that is what they thought I wanted to hear. In fact, he was not what I had thought he was initially; rushing into marriage without knowing him better was my decision too. It is healthier to take ownership of one's situation. This leaves room for me to change my mind if I had wanted to take him back. Friends talking him down made this more difficult.

To consider
1. Criticizing what the person's partner has done may simply make them feel more loyal. How do you criticize the actions but not the person?
2. It's not helpful to stay away because you are embarrassed, or to avoid giving an opinion if asked.

DIVORCE IN THE CHURCH

I have talked with a number of different people about their experiences of divorce and the church. Being a part of the church community appeared to make the situation better and worse. It was better because they were a part of a wider fellowship; it was worse because it left them with a clear sense of what the failure of their marriage meant.

Many Christians are deeply appreciative of the love and support of a church community. Jeanne, a woman I talked with, recounted how, in the difficult months following her divorce when she was coming to terms with life on her own with four children, she was kept going by a church member who simply turned up on the doorstep every morning just before the school run in order to give her a hug. Suzie, who suffered from ME after her divorce, talks warmly of the support that the church was able to give her and her daughter Harriet:

They set up a rota. We had this lovely old lady who lived down the road who went to the church, and she came in every morning—she had a key— and got Harriet up, gave her breakfast and got her ready for school. Then every evening, somebody from church would come round, give her supper and got her to bed. And that's what the church did.

On the other hand, Christians may suffer greater shock because divorce is the last thing they expected. They may struggle with it all the more because, quite simply, it should not be happening. An idea cherished by many Christians is that a Christian marriage is somehow built on a more solid foundation than other marriages, and is thus not likely to founder—but for me this has not been the case. Ironically, at the very time that someone most needs to know they are accepted and loved, they may find themselves cast in the role of the outsider for whom there seems to be no place. Some distancing, either from or by the church community, is inevitable in order for the church to preserve and present the sacramental idea of marriage. Any institution is based on a shared premise about what is right or wrong and the church is no exception. Divorce cuts against both a biblical narrative on the centrality of marriage and a church culture shaped round the assumption of a nuclear family unit. Divorced people in church can find themselves caricatured as 'desperately seeking another partner'. They can be ostracised, seen as a threat to other people's marriages.

A Christian faith may make matters seem worse because it offers a clear picture of what marriage could be, highlighting the contrast of what the divorced person's marriage has become. For Christians, divorce has a special timbre. It has a meaning and significance that is not there for the non-Christian. It violates the sacrament of marriage, which is central to the faith: marriage is the image used to describe the relationship between Christ and the Church (Ephesians 5:31–32). This means that, for a Christian, divorce is not simply about a life choice that didn't work out; it assumes a deeper, spiritual significance. There is a special loss of confidence for someone who has based his life choices on certain principles that now appear to have crumbled.

Peter describes how he felt after his divorce: 'I was wretchedly miserable. I couldn't see any positive future. I had been going to church but I just stopped going. I pretty much lost my faith at that stage, and I felt guilty.'

There is a difference between marriage as a theological ideal and marriage as a social conformity. The theological ideal challenges and delights, while the social conformity judges and dispirits. Aune draws attention to the inherent disadvantages faced by single Christian women due to the gender imbalance within the church.

There are more single women than men in church within all age groups. Overall 68% of evangelical churches are women and only 32% are male. Within the younger age group this division is less pronounced: 56% of singles under thirty are female. As singles get older the imbalance gets greater. In the forty nine to fifty nine age band there are three times more women than men, and for the over sixties women outnumber the male counterparts by six to one. [4]

When churches focus exclusively on teaching about the social conformity of the 'family', single women can feel excluded. Some church leaders do not appear to have cottoned on to the fact that tidy two-parent, two-child families do not exclusively populate their churches. Alice has direct experience of this; she tells the following story:

I remember one Sunday when, as a recently divorced mother with a young daughter, I sat listening to a sermon in which the preacher was talking about the merits of following God's plan for society. To back up his argument, he ran through the UK divorce statistics, then proceeded to cite research on the damaging effects of divorce on children, focusing especially, for some unexplained reason, on the problems absent fathers cause for girls in later life. The sermon was followed by 'a few moments for couples to express their love and appreciation of each other'. When a young couple sitting nearby asked me if I would look after their baby son for a few moments while they took full advantage, I could only shake my head through the tears—whilst feeling mean at having refused them.

One woman, who for many years has attended a large, thriving evangelical church, talked very openly about her experience of an extremely traumatic divorce, and admitted that no one in the church knew she was divorced. Despite knowing that she was surrounded by people who both loved and supported her, she felt quite unable to tell the truth about her situation. Even when divorce is on the table for discussion, it may well be on the church's very particular terms, with the result that people are left feeling like misfits. Karen chose to leave her psychologically abusive husband, and later attended a course on divorce put on by the church. The leaders of the course assumed that everyone attending would have been left by their spouse. As the one who had taken the decision to leave the marriage, she talks about how she felt like an impostor. She explains: 'The course was all based on that assumption. There was no space to say, "Actually, it was me who left..." So the difficulty was, how do you tell that to a Christian group? Because it's just assumed that it's not acceptable.'

Divorced people are a fact and feature of church life—and they are not only people who have joined the church since their divorce. Many have been and will go through the process of separation and divorce while being committed members of a church. As we have noted, Christian faith is no insurance policy against marital breakdown, yet many divorced Christians feel as if they are unacceptable and do not fit the mould. Among some groups of Christians, the words 'Christian' and 'divorce' barely belong in the same sentence. For some, to be divorced and a Christian in the context of church is to wear a label that clearly signals sin and failure.

Simon comments, 'Even though it was not me who had been unfaithful, I felt ashamed. This was not a kosher Christian problem. At that time, no one in my church had been in this situation, and it seemed far outside the bounds of accepted normality.'

To consider
1. How do you help someone to realize that their marriage breakdown is their responsibility without making it feel as if it is their fault?
2. How do you work through your own feelings about divorce?
3. If someone involved in church leadership is getting divorced, can you offer them some kind of sabbatical?
4. How can you help a divorced person to feel that they are still a part of a church fellowship, even if they pull back from the Sunday worship?
5. How can you draw on and support single parents' experiences within the church and other associated events?

✣

FROM RECOGNITION TO
TRANSFORMATION

In this chapter I write my experiences into the framework used by Isaiah to describe the Judeans' attitude towards the coming destruction of Jerusalem. I use the language of the prophet and map the geography of my divorce on to different territories, each one relating to a different period of recovery. Each territory is like a landscape where I come to terms with what has happened and learn to recognize and respond to the God's guidance. According to Christian belief, anything that happens, however painful it might be, can always be drawn into the arena of God's grace and forgiveness, so each of my territories provides a context for the encounter between my experience and God. After Elijah's confrontation with the prophets of Baal, he found God not in the powerful wind or the earthquake or the fire. Instead, God was in the gentle whisper (1 Kings 19:11–13). In my situation, salvation is not going to come from glitzy wine bars or fancy holidays but from a 'still small voice of calm' (in the words of the hymn). My faith tells me that, within each area, understanding the character of God can underpin the process of recovery.

While it may be possible to map the different territories of recovery from divorce, there is no timescale or chronology or order to the process. The emotions are too extreme to allow for a regulated progress. I am constantly drawn back into feelings I thought I had conquered. On occasions, I might begin to feel that I am moving on and getting over what has happened, but then something new strikes me about Sarah's actions and I am catapulted back into feelings of anger and frustration. At other points I am frozen in time, unable to move backwards or forwards. Then my life becomes a perpetual *Groundhog Day*, where the character in the film is forced to live a recurring 24-hour day. As I mentioned in the Introduction, Godard says that a film must have a beginning and a middle and an end but not necessarily in that order. Similarly, the emotions and feelings involved in a divorce cannot be packaged and worked through in a logical and progressive manner. There are different levels of recovery at each stage and each one is continually revisited until eventually each will integrate with the others.

The recurring temptation, during my divorce, is to feel sorry for myself—for my anger to turn into bitterness, my grief to become self-pity and my sense of being hard done by to cause me to feel like a victim. I wrote the following entry in my diary:

I have always had endless sympathy for depression but none for self-pity. Depression is something beyond despair—a country perhaps that lies on the other side of choppy black seas of hopelessness. I had always thought of experiences as things that I learnt and benefited from—the end of a relationship, leaving a job, losing my cheque book, travelling. Everything I had done previously was either telling stories or doing things that I would tell stories about. Now in the space of a year my father has died, my marriage has collapsed and I have been diagnosed with epilepsy. Within twelve months I have lost my health, my wife and my father. It has broken me and I do not have the energy to fight; all I can do is to curl up into a ball and wait. I have gone beyond anger to bitterness but then beyond bitterness to indifference. I am coping because I do not care.

I try to listen for the echo of the life I remember from before; I want to choose life (Deuteronomy 30:19) but I have to find it first. However much I might want to do this, though, there is no automatic pathway towards wholeness. There is an element of snakes and ladders in the process of emotional recovery because there are always feelings that lie in ambush, waiting to pounce. Hence there is a constant need to restart the process of restoration.

Among the longings you have suppressed
And the desires you imagine tamed,
A sweet pain lies in ambush.
BRIAN PATTEN [1]

In order to help me plot my way through the process of recovery, I have identified 'recognition', 'repentance', 'redemption' and 'transformation' as four territories of transition and recovery. The first stage, recognition, is the 'denial' stage of bereavement. This is the point at which there is too much to process and the mind is unable to absorb all that has happened. In a way, it is the kindest stage of the whole process, an anaesthetic against the pain that is to come. At this stage, I am not yet able to come to terms with what has taken place. It is the start of the mapping process. There is an acceptance but not yet an understanding of the reality of the circumstances—acknowledging that the possibility for reconciliation has passed and things will never go back to how they were before.

The second stage, repentance, is the point at which I begin to understand the reality of my situation. I begin the process of deciding which part of it is my responsibility and which part is not. This is the period when I am living through the feelings of anger, hurt, betrayal and failure, but I also begin to realize that there is a shared responsibility for events.

Redemption is more about coming to terms with the situation than about trying to forget Sarah or cut her out of my consciousness. Simply surviving the divorce is a slog and the idea of thinking positively about the future is anathema. The reality of redemption is not in the crisis of what has happened but in the deadness that follows. It is like the period six months after the funeral when the flurry of attention has gone and the mourner is left alone, needing to reconcile herself to the new situation. It is at this point, when everything has settled down, that the silence shouts out.

As I have already said, time is a powerful agent of the Holy Spirit and eventually, when events have taken their course, relationships and circumstances can reshape themselves. This will then offer a final stage for transformation. There is no sudden moment when the suffering is over and new life can begin to take shape; the arrival of a decree absolute through the post is a pathetically inadequate ritual with which to end a marriage. There is a point, though, at which, through a combination of grace, determination and circumstances, thoughts do turn to the future and the desire to learn to live again will come to the fore.

The question of whether suffering is redemptive or destructive recurs as a theme throughout literature. Three novels, Victor Hugo's *Les Miserables*, Dostoevsky's *Crime and Punishment* and William Golding's *Darkness Visible*, and one play, Peter Schaffer's *Equus*, all tell the story of unlikely central characters, each of whom is, in their own way, seemingly damned by their actions and circumstances. These stories ask the same questions of their central characters that I ask of myself. In what way are the characters victims and in what way are they agents of their own situation? How are they affected by and can they move on from what has happened to them?

In *Les Miserables*, Jean Valjean is guilty of breaking his parole. In *Crime and Punishment*, Raskolnikov is guilty of murder. In *Darkness Visible*, Mr Pedigree is a pederast. In *Equus*, Alan Strang has blinded six horses with a spike. The stories look at the struggle between the set of circumstances and the character of the protagonist. This is the question I ask of my divorce: to what extent does the force of events destroy me as a person and to what extent does it shape the person I am to become? In one sense, the plot of each book is a simple variation on the theme 'what does not break you makes you'. In differing degrees, each character goes through the process of recognizing their situation, repenting of their involvement and then seeing the situation redeemed and transformed. I will explore something of their experiences later on in the chapter.

In scripture, Isaiah writes against the background of confusion and the sense of abandonment that the Judeans felt at the collapse of Jerusalem. The book of Isaiah is an invitation to understanding chaos rather than (as, for example, in the book of Job) simply accepting it. The thread running throughout Isaiah is for the survivors to come and reason together (1:18). It is the language of poetry rather than of historical narrative. Isaiah provides a necklace of images that joins together the nature of God and the reality of the situation, asking what is faithful and what is appropriate in a shifting context. In my situation, that context is about struggling in the quagmire of a failed marriage.

RECOGNITION

This is a landscape of havoc and disintegration. Two people hurting each other, tearing apart the vows they have made to each other, splintering their marriage—useless, tatty dreams hanging on the edge of frosty silences, tetchy arguments and misery. Alice, who left her husband after five years of marriage, says the following:

I hated men; I hated married couples; I hated people who were in love; I hated being on the tube where all these couples were kissing each other goodbye… And then I was confronted with saying 'What is this problem I have?' … There were times when I was so angry I could just vomit. I could understand how people become bulimic. I felt so out of control and [as if] I could not do what I wanted to do that I would feel I wanted to be sick.

Peter, who was divorced after nine years of marriage, explains his feelings:

I moved through a number of phases. At first, griefstricken, initially for the loss of the girl I loved as much as for the loss of the marriage. I remember talking to my sister on the phone, and saying 'Why? Why? Why?' And she said, 'You'd better ask her.' But I'm not sure she knew either, really. And then I grieved for the loss of the family. I couldn't stand to watch films where someone got off with someone else's wife. Like Bond films—I had to walk away from it, because I was so upset by the whole thing, about infidelity, and I found it really distressing. I started reading Anna Karenina *and stopped because it was art imitating life—thank you, no... All the money that we have is my money and my family's money, and I've had to give her a great wedge of it because of... very unfair divorce laws. But—are you going to carry on whinging about that all your life? A friend said to me, 'She's been really unfair to you, Peter.' But I've had all this— nah, nah, nah, whinge, whinge, whinge—going on in my head for long enough, and it just eats you up.*

Glimpses of happiness, respect, wholeness, love and laughter are receding. Here, there is nothing more that can be done other than to recognize and be reconciled to the end of the marriage. It is the territory where a person has to begin to accept the reality of the situation.

Divorce is never an isolated phenomenon but comes as a result of a long period of pain and distress. Juliet tells the following story about the break-up of her 15-year marriage:

What led up to the divorce was [that] my husband was working in a nightclub where he took up with a young woman half his age. I found this a tremendous strain. Then he started behaving very violently towards me and one particular dreadful evening, when he tried to strangle me and I thought he was going to succeed, I literally ran out of the house in my nightclothes and didn't go back. I had two children. My son... left the house with me.

I wrote in my own journal:

There is a certain theatricality about my behaviour. I stay with David and Louise, wake up early and stand in front of the mirror shaving the top of my head with a Gillette GII razor. I want to mark the fact that my situation has changed irrevocably. Louise comes in and offers me another razor. She does not say a word further but simply goes to her own bathroom and returns with a clean, sharp, new razor so that I can finish off what I am doing. I appreciate the fact that she does not try to cheer me up. She comforts me because she is acknowledging the reality of what I am going through. I feel that I am trusting the process of life more by abandoning myself to the moment and having the confidence to feel low rather than resolutely looking on the bright side of life.

Later that day I travel to meet my mother and father, who are staying at a hotel in Cambridge. My mother sees me walking towards her— clean shaven, completely bald head, bright yellow jacket, black suede shoes, black trousers and white T-shirt. 'That is awful!' she wails. What she means is that my fashion sense, with bright jacket and shaved head, is awful. I say to her, 'I am afraid it is.' I reply with such passion and sincerity and immediacy that she knows straight away that I am talking about something else.

Isaiah uses a whole succession of different images to illustrate the chaos and destruction facing Jerusalem, and these images and ideas have echoes in my own feelings. I live in the pages of Isaiah: Jerusalem, the city that would not fall, did just that; my marriage, the one that would not fail, did so. The prophet's poetry gives me images with which I can interpret my situation. I do not understand what is happening: I am 'stunned and amazed'; I am blind and sightless. I am 'drunk, but not from wine', I 'stagger, but not from beer' (29:9). I can hear but I cannot understand; I can see but I cannot perceive (6:9). The collapse of my marriage hits me like 'a hailstorm and a destructive wind'; it is like 'a driving rain and a flooding downpour' (28:2). It is 'sheer terror'; 'the bed is too short to stretch out on, the blanket too narrow to wrap around' (vv. 19–20).

I am angry but I fight against resentment as I sit on my own, weekend after weekend. I am hard done by but I fight against feeling like a victim. I am hurt but I fight against self-pity; I am angry but I fight against resentment; I am resentful but I fight against bitterness. Some nights I walk the streets at 3am, waiting for the darkness to pass and the day to begin.

'The grass is withered; the vegetation is gone and nothing green is left' (Isaiah 15:6). I waste away (33:9); I weep and wail bitterly (13:6) and I am drenched with tears (16:9; 22:4). My hands go limp (13:7); I am 'crushed on the threshing floor' (21:10). I am caught by a spirit of dizziness, like a drunkard staggering around in his own vomit (19:14). 'Pangs seize me, like those of a woman in labour' (21:3); I am with child, I writhe in pain, but I give birth to wind (26:18).

Any sense of depression or despair that I might feel, however, is matched by God's reality. Lynch writes that the incarnation has profound implications in terms of the need to act in solidarity with (the pain of) those who suffer.[2] There is comfort in the idea that confusion and chaos are not alien to a God who emptied himself and took on the very nature of a servant in human likeness (Philippians 2:7) and who repeatedly expresses himself through historical revelation. In the Old Testament, God is constantly prepared to see his plans collapse. At the time of Noah, for example, the earth is corrupt and full of violence and God determines to put an end to all people with a flood (Genesis 6:11–13). Each time the harmony of the situation is fragmented, though, there is a leap forward in people's understanding of God. In Isaiah, there appears to be a divine act of self-abnegation, with God allowing the sins of his people to cause the destruction of Jerusalem. The crucifixion appears to be a divine act of self-contradiction. On the cross, the Father gives up the Son as if the Son were a sinner, and the Son gives up the Father as if he is being abandoned (Matthew 27:46). Holy Saturday is the liturgical day of the year for the divorced person because it is the only day in the church's calendar that makes a point of marking separation and isolation without rushing towards resurrection and reconciliation. Christ is in the tomb but not yet risen to the Father.

Extreme experiences will always reshape our view on the world. *Equus* looks at an acute experience of pain and disorder in the story of Alan Strang. The story is told through the eyes of Dysart, a psychiatrist who treats Alan for his mental disorder. During the process of the play, as the reasons for what happened are uncovered, Dysart is drawn towards Alan Strang. He actually even feels jealous of the depth of passion and feeling that led Alan towards the drastic action of blinding the horses:

Dysart: Without worship you shrink, it's as brutal as that... I shrank my own life. No one can do it for you. I settled for being pallid and provincial, out of my own eternal timidity. [3]

The play looks at the way in which Alan's tightly structured social background may have killed a capacity for worship and passion and consequently a capacity for pain. I don't agree with Dysart: sometimes the pain of a situation can be too much and too difficult and not worth the lessons learnt. My voice speaks in the quiet and persistent tone expressed throughout the play by Dysart's friend Hesther: 'The boy is in pain,' she reminds him. 'That's all I see.' I am that boy!

Divorce is an exercise in the grammar of pain. There is nothing glamorous or ennobling about sitting alone on a Saturday night because I have neither energy nor inclination to do anything different. However miserable I am feeling, though, I still hold on to one of the core themes of this book—that divorced people can make a distinctive contribution to the wider mission of the church. The experience of being disenfranchised in such a vivid and brutal manner gives distinctive and valuable insights into the nature of God. Scripture continually hovers round the theme of the outsider and the role the outsider plays in the health and wholeness of the community. My family and friends draw me in during the experience but, equally, I draw them into the new world I am inhabiting.

The suffering servant, without beauty or majesty and with nothing to commend him (Isaiah 53:2), will turn people's eyes towards God. This servant is an intercessor before God, an example of awfulness, an illustration of silent and sincere faith, and his wounds will heal people. There are three ways in which I pick up the mantle of the suffering servant in Isaiah. I am the cautionary example—the failure that demonstrates to his friends the need for them not to take their own marriages for granted. I have a freedom to pray more recklessly than I have ever done before: my own world has collapsed and what is left are those already dear to me. Finally, I am developing a different set of stories from those of my contemporaries who are married with children—there is a vicarious interest on their part for all that I am experiencing.

REPENTANCE

When I move from the landscape of havoc and disintegration, I come to a landscape of accountability. This is a territory where I begin to accept that I had a part to play in the ending of the marriage. I begin to sense God's grace and learn about his judgment. Here begins the process of turning an acknowledgment of my role into a responsibility for the situation, identifying what is and what is not my responsibility in the ending of the marriage and then repenting of the part that has been mine. In many ways, it is more painful than the first stage ('recognition') because I am beginning to understand what I have and have not done, writing myself into the script. I am beginning to realize that I have not been simply a passive participant in an unfortunate set of circumstances, but instead I have been an active contributor to the messy state of affairs.

The idea of repentance brings in its wake the two other key theological themes of sin and forgiveness, considered in more detail elsewhere in this book. Classically, within the Christian tradition, sin is either underestimated or overemphasized. Underplaying sin provides an ethic of relativity. It suggests that what is important is for people to have the right to choose what is best for them. This understanding of sin veers towards the idea that people have a right to happiness, which should be pursued as long as it does not hurt another person. In this instance, although it is 'wrong' to end a marriage, it might be better to do so than to live within an unhappy situation. To underplay sin is a laissez-faire ethos, and it can be quite dangerous.

To overplay sin provides an ethic of absolutism. It suggests that what counts is that people make the right choices, however difficult a situation might be. In this view, it would always be wrong to divorce because marriage is meant to be for life. To overplay sin in this way can be judgmental, legalistic and condemnatory.

Neither of these approaches, underplaying or overplaying, gives me the tools I need to make sense of my situation. One gives me too much responsibility and the other too little. One leaves me struggling to make sense of what has happened; the other leaves me feeling condemned because there was nothing I could do to improve the situation. Instead, I need justice and mercy (Zechariah 7:9) to touch together.

REDEMPTION

The third territory is a landscape of redemption. Redemption is an act of God rather than an act of the will, so it is a territory where I have to be patient and where I learn about God's majesty and holiness. Redemption is different from correction. There is a basic instinct to want to do something to fix a situation, to try to make the situation better—and it is possible to correct but not redeem a situation, simply through effort and determination. Correcting a situation takes planning; redeeming a situation takes patience. Correction an attempt to prevent something going wrong; redemption is dealing with the situation once something has actually happened.

The Bible is a story based on place and location and belonging. It starts in the garden of Eden and culminates in the new Jerusalem. Place is a primary category of faith and land is a central, if not the central, theme of biblical faith. Places also provide the geography for our imagination: our identity is formed, nurtured and fostered by place.[4] London has always been my Jerusalem: it provided the map of my relationship with Sarah. We lived out the dream of the urban promise,[5] living detached, unrooted lives of endless choice and no commitment. Marriage was the value-added package to the lives that each of us would have lived anyway, had we not been married to each other. Marriage was more of a lifestyle option than anything else. This means that there are friends who have only ever known us as a couple, and in London there are houses, restaurants, cinemas, parks and museums where we have been as a couple. There are any number of ways of being happy but there is only one way of being unhappy—on my own—and so I must leave. I change my job and move to a different city to try to escape from the memories we share. I need a new set of noises to listen to and a new group of people to meet.

For Isaiah, place was sacramental because it provided the Israelites with the geography of their relationship with God. In the 'Sound and Light' show at the remains of the Jerusalem temple today, we are told, 'In the middle of the world is the Middle East, in the middle of the Middle East is Jerusalem, in the middle of Jerusalem is the temple, and in the middle of the temple is the Holy of Holies'—and it was there that Isaiah went to meet with God. Angels sang, the doorposts and thresholds shook and Isaiah prostrated himself in fear on the temple floor (Isaiah 6:1–5). The impending disaster for Israel was this loss of place, and the need to learn how to sing the Lord's song in a strange land (Psalm 137) was absolute.

I write in my journal:

I do anything and everything to block out the silences. I wake up to the radio; I go to sleep to music. I develop a finely tuned skill in avoiding being alone with my thoughts. I travel to friends in different parts of the country, sitting in other people's living rooms as a form of social life. I join a gym so that I have something to do at the weekends. I spend as long as I can reading the Saturday and Sunday newspapers, knowing that the rest of the weekend lies ahead of me, empty. I stand in the queue wanting it take longer because, when I reach the front and pay for my purchases, then I will need to think of something else to do. I try to correct the situation by buying new clothes and expensive pens in order to feel better about myself but shopping therapy is no answer to the test of authenticity facing me.

There is no quick-fit solution and the only real choice for me is to find the courage to enter the desert of my loneliness.[6] Rilke helps me to understand this further. He writes:

What is necessary, after all, is only this: solitude, vast inner solitude. To walk inside yourself and meet no one for hours—that is what you must be able to attain. To be solitary as you were when you were a child, when the grown-ups walked around involved with matters that seemed large and important because they looked so busy and because you didn't understand a thing about what they were doing... What is happening in your innermost self is worthy of your entire love.[7]

A sustained period of solitude and reflection is my expression of grief; it is a detachment and a withdrawal from what is happening. By day, I paint a smile on my face; I grit my teeth and I survive. In the evenings and at weekends, when I am on my own, I collapse. To do anything else would be like shutting my eyes, as a child might while watching a horror film, waiting for the scary bits to finish. All I can do is to stop trying to work things out for myself and pretending that life is OK. I have to trust some higher level of possibility ('Trust in the Lord for ever': Isaiah 26:4). It is a part of the curious logic of spirituality that taking hold of a situation means letting it go; giving up means giving over; prayer is an admission of powerlessness as well as an expression of trust and faith in a creator God. I need to stop and wait and listen for the still, small voice of grace. I pray Charles de Foucault's prayer of abandonment:

Father, I abandon myself into your hands; do with me what you will. Whatever you do, I thank you: I am ready for all, I accept all. Let only your will be done in me and in all your creatures. I ask no more than this, O Lord.[8]

Even at this point of faith and absolute abandonment, there is no quick-fit solution. What the Bible calls 'patience' (in spiritual terms), I equate with endurance (in practical terms): everything takes time; feelings and circumstances never get sorted out quickly. All the unseen consequences of a divorce—the damage to one's sense of self, the effect on children and the separating of two lives—can take years to work through.

Les Miserables looks at this issue, exploring how hard it is for a man to redeem his life from his past misdeeds. Jean Valjean, the hero of the story, determines to escape from his past and redeem his life but he is caught by the consequences of what he has done. Here, the scenery blends repentance into redemption. Jean Valjean steals a silver goblet from a priest with whom he has been given accommodation for the night while on parole. He is caught by the police and brought back with the stolen goblet. Instead of being put in prison, however, he is set free when the priest says that the only reason Valjean took the goblet is that he himself had given it to him.

The Bishop had spoken the words slowly and deliberately. He concluded with a solemn emphasis: Jean Valjean, my brother, you no longer belong to what is evil but to what is good. I have bought your soul to save it from black thoughts and the spirit of perdition, and I give it to God.[9]

The story then follows Valjean's desire to redeem his life in response to what the priest has done. Until the end of the book, however, he is unable to escape from Inspector Javert, who is determined to see him back in prison for an earlier infringement he had committed while on parole. Valjean has repented but Javert still wants to see him suffer the consequences of his actions. At the crucial point of the story, Javert is in a position to arrest Valjean. Javert recognizes that Valjean has fully atoned for his earlier misdeeds and he elects not to arrest him. Valjean is free but Javert, the agent of the law, can't let go of his feelings. He is condemned by his own logic of judgment, which has now been overtaken by the claims of mercy.

It is at the point of crisis that people reveal their truest selves. Jesus shows his identity most clearly at points of rejection. He has full authority to take up or to lay down his life (John 10:18) and he still chooses to move away from Galilee, to go to Jerusalem, where he knows that he will face death. He then waits until he is on trial and about to be killed before he makes his clearest and only direct claim to be the Messiah (Mark 14:62). It is at this moment, when he is most exposed and vulnerable, that he is clearest about his identity.

There are times when people dictate events and there are times when events dictate to people. This is what is meant by Jesus' passion. Vanstone talks of the passion as Jesus' period of waiting. 'Passion' means being 'done to' rather than 'doing'—there is no immediate connotation in the word of pain and suffering. Vanstone also explains the pivotal significance in the Gospels of Jesus being handed over to the authorities (Mark 14:53). Jesus' situation is now one of dependence, exposure and waiting, being no longer in control of the situation, being the object of what is done: 'He passes from doing to receiving what others do, from working to waiting, from the role of subject to that of object and in the proper sense of the phrase from action to passion.'[10]

In *Crime and Punishment*, the climax of the book comes when Sonia is waiting for Raskolnikov's release from prison. Raskolnikov, the antihero, had rationalized that the murder of an old woman money lender would be justified on the basis that it would provide him with the money needed to finish his studies. However, the reality does not match the theory and he is haunted by what he has done in killing her. He becomes the lover of Sonia, who is a prostitute. Sonia (the Christ figure in the story) loves him and eventually persuades him to confess to the police what he has done. He is taken away to Siberia, where Sonia follows him and patiently waits for his prison sentence to run its course. She waits near the prison fence to talk with him and bring him gifts during his daily hour of exercise. Although she is happy to wait, he is scornful of her devotion to him. It is only when Sonia is ill and unable to visit that he finds himself missing her and waiting with anxious concern— and it is at this point, when he realizes that he is waiting for her, that he also realizes he loves her. At the end of the book, there is a moment of enlightenment in which Raskolnikov realizes that Sonia truly loves him and will wait for him during the time he is in prison.

They tried to speak but were unable to. There were tears in their eyes. Both of them looked pale and thin; but in these ill, pale faces there now gleamed the dawn of a renewed future, a complete recovery to a new life. What had revived them is love, the heart of one containing an infinite source of life for the heart of the other… They determined to wait and endure. There were still seven years to go, and until that time is over how much unendurable torment and how much infinite happiness they would experience! But he had recovered and he knew it, felt it completely with the whole of his renewed being, while she—she, after all, lived only in his life![11]

The process of seeing a situation redeemed is long and slow. This process, gradually and slowly, then turns into a landscape of holiness and obedience.

TRANSFORMATION

Can anything good come out of Nazareth (John 1:46)? Can anything worthwhile come out of a divorce? The fourth and final view is of a territory only touched as yet. It is a landscape of transformation, a place where I am no longer defined by the awfulness of what has happened. There is no longer any need to be brittle, angry and defensive. I live among the ruins of my marriage and in the middle of chaos and disorder but I can now look beyond and see glimpses of God's transcendence. Redemption is about saving something from the wreckage, whereas transformation is when I walk away and leave the wreckage behind: 'I let go of the rage and sorrow… when I could finally see again I saw the first rays of day reflected in the murky river… This is not judgment day but only morning, morning pale fair and excellent.'[12]

Experience has reshaped my sense of identity and I have begun to feel secure in my misery. When the prospect of happiness reappears, I will think nostalgically back on what I will remember as my hibernation period. When the prospect of joy reappears, however, beckoning like a long-forgotten friend, my temptation will be to hold on to my reeds of unhappiness. They are serving me well, giving me experiences, insights and understanding that I would never otherwise have had. Yet I do not want to be the guest at the wedding feast thrown into the outer darkness for not wearing a wedding garment (Matthew 22:12–13). In my journal I write a short poem:

There
are
friends,
people
and
places
to
help
you
to
forget.

The
pity
is
that
they
succeed.

If I can walk away from the worst of all that has taken place, then maybe it was never so bad after all? Happiness is kind and comforting but complicated. Isaiah tantalizes me with the possibility that the Israelites' suffering is not only redemptive but also transformative: not only will there be a new heaven and a new earth (Isaiah 65:17), but all that Israel has endured will be part of the process leading there. Divorce will reshape me: events that were previously a part of the tapestry of a marriage are now quoted in lawyers' documents as evidence of its breakdown. Shared experiences, that previously built the two of us up, now condemn the marriage as a failure. Isaiah's alluring suggestion is that these experiences will change shape again and be part of a restoration to wholeness. The stone that caused me to stumble will be the one thing that helps me to work through the situation (Isaiah 8:14). I will be repaid for the years the locusts have eaten (Joel 2:25).

PRAYERS FOR SEPARATION

These prayers are taken from *Vows and Partings*, Methodist Publishing House, 2001.

1. When a marriage has ended in divorce
2. When someone has walked out
3. Being separate
4. Seeking forgiveness
5. Seeking forgiveness from another person
6. How can I begin to forgive myself?
7. Ending of a close relationship
8. A prayer affirming the good things in a previous relationship
9. When a relationship intended to lead to marriage has ended
10. A prayer for my partner at the ending of our relationship
11. Prayers for other family members affected by separation

✣

WHEN A MARRIAGE HAS ENDED IN DIVORCE

Gracious God,
We remember before you a marriage that began with high hopes.
We give thanks for the years of joy and security
Which this partnership has brought
And for the love given and received.
Now we place before you the times that have been impossible,
The hearts that have grown cold
And the feelings that cannot be resolved.
You are a God of healing and forgiveness
And we pray that bitterness may not sour our future
Nor unresolved issues burn within us.
We pray that you will continue to bless and guide in separation
Those who once stood before you as one.
Because none can ever fall from your caring love
Keep each of us safe,
And because you alone know everything about us
Heal each of our wounds.
These things we ask through our Lord and Saviour Jesus Christ.
Amen

Gracious God,
You called us to live in harmony
And to reflect your perfect love;
Yet despite our sincerely made promises
And all our best endeavours
We confess that we have failed you
And failed each other.

We pray for those most affected
By the end of our marriage,
For our children, our family and our friends,
That they may be spared further hurt
And that we may not lose their ongoing love.
And we pray for ourselves,
That you will save us
From all resentment and bitterness,
And give us strength to rebuild our lives.
God of grace,
Forgive us what is past,
Help us as we struggle with the present,
And guide us into the future;
For the sake of Jesus Christ our Lord. **Amen**

O Lord, we pray for those who, full of confidence and love, once chose a partner for life and are now alone after a final separation. May they receive the gift of time, so that hurt and bitterness may be redeemed by healing and love, personal weakness by your strength, inner despair by the joy of knowing you and serving others; through Jesus Christ our Lord. **Amen**

✠

WHEN SOMEONE HAS WALKED OUT

Lord Jesus,
You know what it is like for someone to walk out:
You were betrayed and deserted by your friends.
Like them, N has gone without a word of explanation.
What am I to think?
Has she/he gone to get away from me
Or to be with someone else?
Will she/he, like Peter, deny the one she/he has known?
What shall I do with all these things left unresolved?
Will we meet again?
Is there any chance of reconciliation?
Lord Jesus,
Help me to know that you are with me, and do not abandon me
in my darkness. **Amen**

✣

BEING SEPARATE

Lord,
There is much in my mind that has healed,
But still there is pain in my heart.
I do not always feel forgiven or forgiving:
Wounds still hurt and doubts remain.

I prefer a life with no remainders
And situations with no loose ends.

Help me to understand that life is not like that.

May I find the place in my life where I can move on,
Where I can be cleansed from previous bitterness,
And where I can be set free from recurring passions
That torment my spirit. **Amen**

✣

SEEKING FORGIVENESS

God of mercy and compassion,
Forgive me for the hurt I have caused to those I have loved.
Forgive the angry words, the bitter thoughts,
The resentment that wells up within me.
Forgive me when others have been caught up in our arguments:
Friends, parents, children.
Help me to learn how to forgive as I live with my regrets.
Help me to restore relationships
With those whose trust in me has been damaged. **Amen**

✠

SEEKING FORGIVENESS
FROM ANOTHER PERSON

God of mercy,
Give me strength to seek the forgiveness of the one I have hurt.

As I confess to them words spoken in anger,
Each one a weapon intended to wound;
As I recall in their presence actions rooted in self-interest,
Every one a sign that the one I loved meant nothing to me;
As I remember before them silences kept,
Preventing our frail attempts to communicate,
Intentionally undermining confidence;

God of mercy,
Give me strength to seek the forgiveness of the one I have hurt.

As I confess to them that there were better and more helpful
ways in which to have parted;
as I recall in their presence suffering and pain that I could have
relieved, if I had acted differently;
as I remember before them how I attacked them so aggressively,
in order to defend the depth of my feelings;

God of mercy,
Give me strength to seek the forgiveness of the one I have hurt.

✛

HOW CAN I BEGIN TO FORGIVE MYSELF?

Gracious God,
How can I begin to forgive myself?
Your promise is to forgive all who truly repent.
I regret what has happened and confess my part in it,
Yet every day, I wake up remembering—
And my guilt is a heavy weight.
Others may forgive me,
and assure that you forgive me too,
but the dark clouds of my guilt block out the light of your love.

How can I begin to forgive myself?

When Jesus came face to face with Peter at the lakeside,
He asked, 'Do you love me?'
I long to hear that question and to answer
 'Yes, Lord, you know that I love you,'
but my guilt is a barrier between us.

Help me to hear the voice of the risen Lord,
To accept your forgiveness
And to forgive myself. **Amen**

✠

ENDING OF A CLOSE RELATIONSHIP

Gracious God,
We remember our years together,
In which we have grown and changed.
We pray for each other as we separate.
May we be enriched by our happy memories
And let go of our painful ones.
Bless us both in our life journeys,
And give us confidence to walk into the future
Strengthened by the time we have shared,
And with each other's blessing. **Amen**

✢

A PRAYER AFFIRMING THE GOOD THINGS IN A PREVIOUS RELATIONSHIP

Gracious God,
Even when our hopes are left unfulfilled and our fears are realized,
we know that your goodness and mercy have followed us all
the days of our life.
We remember before you all that was good in A and C's
relationship:
The happy times they shared;
The commitments they maintained;
The pleasures they enjoyed;
The difficulties they overcame;
The friends they made;
The interests they shared;
The home they established;
The places they visited;
The challenges they met;
 (The children they love;)

For these and all your blessings to A and C we give you thanks
and praise
Through Jesus Christ our Lord. **Amen**

Loving God,
As I grieve for the relationship that has now ended
Help me to give thanks for all that was good
Without clinging to the past;
Help me to put aside all that was hurtful,
Not allowing bitterness to cloud the present;
Above all, help me to look to the future with hope
And believe in the possibility of a new beginning. **Amen**

✣

WHEN A RELATIONSHIP INTENDED TO LEAD TO MARRIAGE HAS ENDED

God of all goodness and source of love,
We give you our thanks and praise
For the times of love and happiness
And the seasons of peace and contentment,
Which the bonds of this friendship and companionship
have brought.
We recall the foundations laid and the plans forged.
But now we remember before you with sorrow the days of
Darkness and difficulty that love could not sustain
And the misunderstandings that devotion could not resolve.
In your mercy forgive us
And in your love heal our hearts and memories.
Bless each of us in our separation
And, wherever we go,
Keep us safe in the arms of your goodness and love;
Through Jesus Christ our Lord. **Amen**

✣

A PRAYER FOR MY PARTNER AT THE ENDING OF OUR RELATIONSHIP

God our healer,
As I pray for N,
I ask that you will help her/him at this time of change.
May she/he go aware that she/he goes with my blessing.
Help her/him to remember all that we enjoyed together
And to put aside unhappy and unhelpful memories.
As our special relationship ends may our friendship remain. **Amen**

✙

PRAYERS FOR OTHER FAMILY MEMBERS AFFECTED BY SEPARATION

Merciful God,
In disappointment and bewilderment
We turn to you.

We knew everything wasn't right,
But we never dreamt it would come to this.
Is there something we should have said?
Something more we could have done?

Open our ears to listen to both A and C,
And our hearts to share their pain.
Help us to understand and support them
And not to rush into judgment.

Whatever the future holds,
May what we think and say and do
Be filled with the love and compassion
Of Jesus Christ our Lord. **Amen**

✧

NOTES

INTRODUCTION

1   M. Crossley, *Introducing Narrative Psychology: Self, Trauma and the Construction of Meaning*, OUP, 2000.

2   E. Kübler-Ross, *On Death and Dying*, Macmillan, 1969.

3   A. Williams, 'Pierrot in Context' in D. Wills (ed.) *Jean-Luc Godard's Pierrot le Fou*, CUP, 2000, p. 44.

4   Leo Tolstoy, *Anna Karenina*, Penguin Classics, 2003, chapter 1.

5   S. Pattison, *Shame: Theory, Therapy, Theology*, CUP, 2000.

6   The Church of England General Synod, 09/07/02.

7   E. Beck-Gernsheim, *Reinventing the Family*, Polity Press, 2002, pp. 18, 24.

8   A. Thatcher, *Theology and Families*, Blackwell, 2007, p. 19.

9   C. Myss, *Why People Don't Heal and How They Can*, Bantam, 1997.

LIVING IN EXILE

1   P. Taylor, *The Texts of Paulo Freire*, OUP, 1993, p. 62.

2   W. Brueggeman, *The Prophetic Imagination*, Augsburg Fortress, 2001, p. 66.

3   W. Brueggeman, *Hopeful Imagination*, Fortress Press, 1986, p. 2.

4   W. Golding, *Darkness Visible*, Faber & Faber, 1980, p. 14.

5   N.T. Wright, *The Resurrection*, SPCK, 2003, p. 478.

6   Ibid., p. 358.

7   Ibid., p. 737.

8   J. Inge, *A Christian Theology of Place*, Ashgate, 2003, p. 49.

9   W. Brueggeman, *The Land*, Fortress Press, 2002.

10   W. Brueggeman, *Hopeful Imagination*, p. 96.

11   B. Okri, *The Famished Road*, Jonathan Cape, 1991.

12   E. Wiesel, 'Longing for home' in L. Buechner (ed.), *The Longing for Home*, University of Notre Dame Press, 1996, p. 19.

13   J. Fortunato, (1987) *Aids: the Spiritual Endeavour*, Harper & Row, 1987, p. 33.

14   V. Bauman, (1993) *Postmodern Ethics*, Blackwell, 1993.

15   Brueggeman, *Hopeful Imagination*, pp. 43, 23.

16   Ibid., pp. 15, 25.

17   W. Brueggeman, *A Commentary on Jeremiah—Exile and Homecoming*, Eerdmans, 1998, p. 29.

18   W. Golding, *The Spire*, Faber & Faber, 2005.

19   Brueggeman, *A Commentary on Jeremiah*, p. 78.

20   D. Robertson, *Marriage—Restoring Our Vision*, BRF, 2005.

21   G. Wenham & W. Heth, *Jesus and Divorce*, Paternoster, 2002, pp. 198–200.

22   O. Wilde, *The Importance of Being Earnest*, Penguin Popular Classics, 1995.

23   A. Macintyre, *After Virtue*, Duckworth, 1990.

24   S. Wells, *Improvisation: The Drama of Christian Ethics*, SPCK, 2004.

25   R. Williams, *A Ray of Darkness*, Cowley Publications, 1995, p. 149.

26   Ibid., p. 121.

27   H. Nouwen, *The Wounded Healer*, DLT, 2001, p. 83.

28   H. Nouwen, *The Return of the Prodigal*, DLT, 1996, p. 13.

29   Brueggeman, *The Prophetic Imagination*, pp. 39–40.

30   Brueggeman, *Hopeful Imagination*, pp. 103, 110.

31   L. Newbigin, *Open Secret*, Eerdmans, 1978, p. 163.

32   Brueggeman, *Hopeful Imagination*, p. 115.

33   W. Shakespeare, *Hamlet*, Act V, Scene 2.

THEOLOGICAL CRAVINGS

1   S. Pattison, *Shame: Theory, Therapy, Theology*, CUP, 2000, p. 200.
2   Ibid., p. 43.
3   J. Young, *The Cost of Certainty*, DLT, 2004, p. 156.
4   P. Tillich, *The Courage to Be*, Yale University Press, 2000.
5   Pattison, *Shame*, p. 144.
6   Ibid., p. 248.
7   Ibid., p. 245.
8   Nouwen, *The Wounded Healer*, p. 33.
9   A. Jamieson, J. Mcintosh, A. Thompson, *Church Leavers: Faith Journeys Five Years On*, SPCK, 2006.
10 S. Griffiths, *God of the Valley*, BRF, 2003, p. 64.
11 K. Barth, *Evangelical Theology*, Eerdmans, 1963, p. 134.
12 Brueggeman, *Hopeful Imagination*, pp. 79, 72.
13 G. Hull, *Equal to Serve: Women and Men in the Church and Home*, Fleming H. Revell, 1987, p. 115.
14 A. Spencer, *Beyond the Curse: Women Called to Ministry*, Thomas Nelson, 1985, p. 45.
15 S. Hauerwass, *Cross Shattered Christ*, DLT, 2004, p. 15.
16 Pattison, *Shame*, p. 280.
17 E. Brunner, *The Mediator*, Lutterworth Press, 1934, p. 488.
18 M. Volf, *Free of Charge*, Zondervan, 2005, pp. 129–30, 170.
19 H. Mackintosh, *The Christian Experience of Forgiveness*, Nisbet, 1927, p. 129.
20 H. Williams, in W.H. Vanstone, *Love's Endeavour, Love's Expense*, DLT, 1977, p. xi.
21 www.theforgivenessproject.com
22 Volf, *Free of Charge*.

THE FAMILY

1   Thatcher, *Theology and Families*, p. 202.

2   V. George & P. Wilding, *British Society and Social Welfare*, Macmillan, 1999, p. 63.

3   J. Drane & O. Fleming-Drane, *Family Fortunes: Faithful Caring for Today's Families*, DLT, 2004, p. 22.

4   S. Hayman, *Step Families: Surviving and Thriving in a New Family*, Simon Schuster, 2005, p. 2.

5   S. Mol, 'Symptoms of post-traumatic stress disorder after non-traumatic events: evidence from an open population study', *The British Journal of Psychiatry* (2005) 186:494–499.

6   J. Williams, quoted in *The Times*, 12 May 2004.

7   Drane & Fleming-Drane, *Family Fortunes*, p. 32.

8   B. Neale, J. Flowerdew, T. Sanders, *Parent Problems 2: Looking Back at Our Parents' Divorce*, Young Voice, 2004.

9   Thatcher, *Theology and Families*, p. 133.

10 Beck-Gernsheim, *Reinventing the Family*, p. 34.

11 www.divorce-online.co.uk, accessed June 2005.

12 P. Wilson, *Being Single*, DLT, 2005, p. 60.

13 George & Wilding, *British Society and Social Welfare*.

14 U. Beck & E. Beck-Gernsheim, *The Normal Chaos of Love*, Polity, 1995.

15 George & Wilding, *British Society and Social Welfare*, p. 63.

16 www.divorce-online.co.uk, June 2005.

17 Beck-Gernsheim, *Reinventing the Family*, p. 7.

18 Thatcher, *Theology and Families*, p. 31.

19 Z. Bauman, *Liquid Modernity*, Polity Press, 2000.

20 H. Kirwan-Taylor, www.dailymail.co.uk/pages/live/femail/article, accessed 2 May 2007.

21 *Living in Britain: Results from the General Household Survey*, Office for National Statistics, Stationery Office, 1998.

22 A.R. Poortman, *Women's Work and Divorce: A Matter of Anticipation? A Research Note*, June 2005.

23 B. Geldof, 'The Real Love that Dare not Speak its Name' in A. Bainham, B. Lindley, M. Richards (eds.), *Children and Their Families*, Hart Publishing, 2003.

24 Hayman, *Step Families*, p. 4.

25 E. Marquardt, *Between Two Worlds: The Inner Lives of Children of Divorce*, Crown, 2005.

26 Hayman, *Step Families*.

27 S. Katzenberg, *I Want a Divorce*, Kyle Cathie, 1999.

28 M. Lawler, 'Towards a Theology of a Christian Family', *INTAMS Review*, 2002.

29 E. Simpson, *Get a Single Life*, Hodder & Stoughton, 2005.

30 J. Chandler, M. Williams, M. Maconachie, T. Collett, B. Dodgeon, B. (2004) 'Living Alone: Its Place in Household Formation and Change', *Sociological Research Online*, 2004, Volume 9, Issue 3.

31 Thatcher, *Theology and Families*, p. 202.

32 K. Cox & M. Desforges, *Children and Divorce: a Guide for Adults*, National Society/Church House Publishing, 1997.

33 N. Hornby, *About a Boy*, Penguin, 2000, pp. 270, 271.

34 M. Foucault, *Madness and Civilisation*, Tavistock, 1979.

35 Ibid., p. 288.

36 Ibid., p. 287.

DOS AND DON'TS

1 E. Kübler-Ross, *On Grief and Grieving: Finding the Meaning of Grief through the Five Stages of Loss*, Scribner, 2005.

2 H. Williams, *True Resurrection*, Pitman Press, 1972, p. 140.

3 H. Nouwen, *Reaching Out*, Ave Maria Press, 1975.

4 K. Aune, *Single Women: A Challenge to the Church*, Paternoster, 2002, p. 17.

FROM RECOGNITION TO TRANSFORMATION

1   B. Patten, 'The Ambush' in *Love Poems*, Flamingo, 1981.
2   G. Lynch, *Understanding Theology and Popular Culture*, Blackwell, 2005, p. 105.
3   P. Schaffer, *Equus*, Penguin, 1973, p. 82.
4   Inge, *A Christian Theology of Place*, p. 130.
5   W. Brueggeman, *The Land*, Fortress Press, 2002.
6   Nouwen, *The Return of the Prodigal Son*, p. 13.
7   R.M Rilke, *Letters to a Young Poet*, Vintage Books, 1987.
8   C. de Foucault, *Madness and Civilisation*, Tavistock, 1979.
9   V. Hugo, *Les Miserables*, Penguin, 1986, p. 111.
10 W. Vanstone, *The Stature of Waiting*, DLT, 1994, p. 31.
11 F. Dostoevsky, *Crime and Punishment*, Penguin, 1991, p. 629.
12 W. Styron, *Sophie's Choice*, Vintage, 2005, p. 632.

✠

MARRIAGE—RESTORING OUR VISION

DAVID ROBERTSON

This book aims to restore our vision of God's created purpose for marriage. It allows the Bible to shed light on both our inherited cultural values and our contemporary Christian assumptions. Linking with the vows in the Marriage Service, it examines biblical principles and challenges current practice. The author also unpacks difficult issues such as cohabitation, divorce and remarriage.

Entertaining, thought provoking and stimulating, this book can be read by an individual, or used with groups as a basis for a Bible study or teachng series. The ideas and images used will communicate clearly to young and old, whether single, married or divorced. For all those wanting to think about the subject, it will help them to discover God's pattern for married life.

ISBN 978 1 84101 402 9   £7.99
Available from your local Christian bookshop or, in case of difficulty, direct from BRF using the order form on page 175.

✠

RE-EMERGING CHURCH

Strategies for reaching a returning generation

ROGER STANDING

When people return to church for the first time in years, are congregations ready to welcome them? One of the largest generational groups ever, the 'Baby Boomers', are now approaching retirement, when questions of spirituality, life and death often resurface. This was the last generation for whom 'Sunday school' was a normal part of childhood—so reconnecting with church may be tinged with nostalgia. At the same time, Baby Boomers grew up in an era of unprecedented personal choice and increasingly sophisticated consumer attitudes, so how can churches help them feel at home while still engaging them with a clear gospel message?

This book discusses how congregations and leaders alike can be prepared for reaching out to those rediscovering Christianity, or at least giving church a try again. It raises relevant pastoral issues, illustrated by fictional case studies, as well as exploring what Christians can do to ensure that their worship—and their church life in general—is a place where new shoots of faith can grow.

ISBN 978 1 84101 492 0 £7.99
Available from your local Christian bookshop or, in case of difficulty, direct from BRF using the order form on page 175.

✣

LIVING IN GRACE

Virtue Ethics and Christian living

CLAIRE DISBREY

In recent years, the Church's witness has been overshadowed at times by its struggles with painful ethical controversies, facing apparently stark choices between 'keeping the law' or 'doing what love demands'. At the same time, in our post-Christian, multi-faith culture, we urgently need to find common ground on which to base shared values for society. Can the Bible help us in these circumstances? Is it the ultimate book of rules to be obeyed—or is it telling us simply to follow 'the way of love'? Can we take the biblical call to holiness seriously without becoming modern-day Pharisees and respond to the awesome responsibility of the Christian's radical freedom from living under the law?

This book looks at people in real, complex life situations and at specific passages from the New Testament, and demonstrates how the teaching of both Jesus and the apostle Paul reveals a third way, transcending both legalism and a kind of hedonism. It shows how the ancient, rediscovered notion of Virtue Ethics can help lead us through hard personal decisions and painful ethical dilemmas.

ISBN 978 1 84101 403 6   £7.99
Available from your local Christian bookshop or, in case of difficulty, direct from BRF using the order form on page 175.

✣

MENTORING FOR SPIRITUAL GROWTH

Sharing the journey of faith

TONY HORSFALL

This book is an introduction to spiritual mentoring, for those who are exploring this aspect of discipleship or embarking on training for ministry as a mentor within their church. Over recent years the ancient Christian practice of spiritual direction has become increasingly popular, as more and more people from every part of the Church seek to know God more deeply. Terms such as 'mentoring' and 'soul' or 'spiritual' friendship are also being used to describe the process of one person coming alongside another to help them grow as a disciple of Jesus.

Tony Horsfall is an experienced spiritual mentor, and in this accessible book he explains through the metaphor of the journey both process and purpose—what mentoring means, its benefits to all involved, and how to explore the call to be a mentor to others. Written primarily for those unfamiliar with the whole area of spiritual direction, it will encourage you to prioritize your own spiritual growth as well as consider whether God may be calling you to be a 'soul friend'.

ISBN 978 1 84101 562 0   £7.99
Available from your local Christian bookshop or, in case of difficulty, direct from BRF using the order form on page 175.

✣

CRYING FOR THE LIGHT

Bible readings and reflections for living with depression

VERONICA ZUNDEL

'This book is not a self-help book, a medical textbook or a complete guide to depression or mental illness. There are plenty of books already to do that. It is more of an attempt to tell one Christian's story, to hear the voices of others with similar experiences, and to discover whether the Bible can both echo our experiences and play a part in healing our wounds.'

Crying for the Light draws on Veronica Zundel's experiences—over nearly 35 years—of clinical depression. As well as sharing her own story, she explores the particular challenges faced by Christians going through such times. Turning to the Bible, she offers reflections on 28 relevant passages, interspersed with meditative prayers from members of Waving not Drowning, an online community set up by Veronica to provide mutual support, information and prayer for people with depression. A concluding resources section includes details of helpful organizations, web resources and books.

ISBN 978 1 84101 565 1 £5.99
Available from your local Christian bookshop or, in case of difficulty, direct from BRF using the order form on page 175.

ORDER FORM

REF	TITLE	PRICE	QTY	TOTAL
402 9	*Marriage—Restoring Our Vision*	£7.99		
492 0	*Re-emerging Church*	£7.99		
403 6	*Living in Grace*	£7.99		
562 0	*Mentoring for Spiritual Growth*	£7.99		
565 1	*Crying for the Light*	£5.99		

POSTAGE AND PACKING CHARGES						
Order value	UK	Europe	Surface	Air Mail	Postage and packing:	
£7.00 & under	£1.25	£3.00	£3.50	£5.50	Donation:	
£7.01–£30.00	£2.25	£5.50	£6.50	£10.00	**Total enclosed:**	
Over £30.00	free	prices on request				

Name _____ Account Number _____

Address _____

_____ Postcode _____

Telephone Number _____ Email _____

Payment by: ☐ Cheque ☐ Mastercard ☐ Visa ☐ Postal Order ☐ Maestro

Card no. ☐☐☐☐ ☐☐☐☐ ☐☐☐☐ ☐☐☐☐

Expires ☐☐ ☐☐ Security code ☐☐☐ Issue no. ☐☐☐

Signature _____ Date _____

All orders must be accompanied by the appropriate payment.

Please send your completed order form to:
BRF, 15 The Chambers, Vineyard, Abingdon OX14 3FE
Tel. 01865 319700 / Fax. 01865 319701 Email: enquiries@brf.org.uk

☐ Please send me further information about BRF publications.

Available from your local Christian bookshop.   BRF is a Registered Charity

Resourcing your spiritual journey

through...

- Bible reading notes
- Books for Advent & Lent
- Books for Bible study and prayer
- Books to resource those working with under 11s in school, church and at home

- Quiet days and retreats
- Training for primary teachers and children's leaders
- Godly Play
- Barnabas RE Days

For more information, visit the **brf** website at **www.brf.org.uk**